ACKNOWLEDGMENTS

No man is an island, and no one stands where he is due solely to his own efforts. I am grateful for the tutelage of many great masters in many fields, and they are too many to recall in this space. I wish to single out, however, a few significant names.

I would like to express my gratitude for the coaching and instruction of Mike Koenigs, Ed Rush, and Pam Hendrickson, without whom I would not have accomplished what I set out to do. I am grateful for the inspiration and friendship afforded me by my close friend and client, Frank Leyes, who has helped me learn more lessons than I might care to admit.

I am forever in the debt of my best friend, business partner, and brother in Christ, John Riding, whose untimely passing forced me to move forward in his absence. John, your leadership and friendship have brought me to this place. I am also indebted to his wife, Leicia, whose kindness and support have been a great comfort.

I am grateful for the support, patience, and tolerance of my team at Ignite Press, who continue to make me look better than I deserve. For Malia Sexton, Publishing Coordinator, for Kyle Relph, Videographer and A/V Engineer, for Samantha Maxwell, Chief Editor, and especially for Karen O'Keefe, my Bookkeeper and mother.

I could do nothing without the ongoing support of my family and especially my dear wife, Carrie, who has continued to have confidence in my crazy entrepreneurial notions. And I am grateful for my children, Connor, Claire, and Kyle, who have continued to look up to me even when I did not deserve it.

Finally and ultimately, I am grateful for my Savior, without whom I would receive what I actually deserve.

DEDICATION

This book is dedicated to the creative, driven, and passionate entrepreneur in all of us. May this book inspire you to take the most powerful step into your future.

Table of Contents

PREFACE

I suspect three types of people will read this book. See if you fall into one of these categories:

1. You are early in your current field, and you are motivated to build your business or brand far more rapidly than your competition. You understand that being perceived as an expert in your field would make a huge difference in the trajectory of your business.
2. You have an established business, but you know you could dramatically improve your business given the proper tools and strategies. You recognize the value of differentiation and what this could mean for your future.
3. You have already built a thriving business, and you want to use the next period to pass on your knowledge to others, to leave an impact on those around you. You are getting ready to make a transition and recognize that you have a message you would like to share with the world.

Well, I said three types, but there really is a fourth type of person with whom I regularly work:

You have learned a great deal in your life, and you want to leave a legacy for those around you. You are less concerned about making money and more concerned about sharing your message with the world. For you, it is all about impact and legacy.

Do you see yourself in one of these four descriptions? I have worked with all four types to help them become authors. In fact, I have helped them become Amazon #1 bestselling authors. If you are so inclined, I can do the same for you!

In fact, if you suspect you would benefit from having a book, feel free to reach out to me right now. I would be happy to meet with you briefly via phone or video conference to discuss your situation. You can visit https://IgnitePress.us to schedule a complimentary book consultation.

Don't know what you would write? We can discuss your desired outcome and your target market first and *then* determine the best topic for your book. Our proven writing process makes book creation both rapid and successful.

Now let's get busy!

INTRODUCTION

In March of 2013, I had a number of new experiences. I wrote my first book, *The Video Tractor Beam*. I also *published* my first book. And for the first time in my life, I saw my name online next to some of the biggest names in publishing.

I remember the morning I first saw my name on Amazon. I had submitted all my book files to Amazon some time before. Ever since, I had been searching Amazon for my name, hoping to discover myself there. And then, it happened. I wrote my name in the search bar, hit enter, and was greeted with one of the most memorable sights I will ever encounter online.

There, below the orange Amazon logo, was the striking blue cover of *The Video Tractor Beam*. Next to that was my name. My heart leapt. Although I had done all the work to make this happen, it still seemed incomprehensible that my name and my book would be present on the world's largest online book store.

Let me help you understand what this feels like.

Imagine for a moment you are at an event. Perhaps it is a wedding or an awards banquet, and they are showing a slideshow or video montage. What do you do? You automatically start searching for people you recognize in the video. More than that, you probably start looking for yourself. That's normal; you are hardwired to do this. When you finally see yourself, what feeling goes through your mind? You might tell me you are embarrassed about some perceived flaw you think you have.

You might feel a bit uncomfortable because of your pose or your attire. But if you are honest with yourself, I imagine you also feel some sense of pride that you are included in the presentation. Your search to find yourself there has ended successfully, and you find yourself encouraged and pleased.

Take that feeling and multiply it times a million!

Seeing your name, book cover, and your image on Amazon for the first time is an *exquisite* experience. For most people, there is a simultaneous feeling of joy and accomplishment, along with a swelling of pride. And this isn't the ugly pride that says, "I am better than everyone else or above everyone else." It is the pride of having done something both difficult and rare: the good kind of pride.

Now back to my story. This feeling of pride, this sense of accomplishment, was just the beginning of a series of pleasant and powerful surprises. More were to unfold as we launched the book.

In the days leading up to our book launch, my co-author and I worked hard to get the word out among friends and family. We basically asked everyone we knew, or even *used to* know, to buy our book. We made phone calls, sent emails, made Facebook posts, and more, all designed to help our book became a bestseller for a time.

When launch day arrived and people started buying our book, we had a bit of a gut check. For several hours, though we knew people were buying, we saw no movement on Amazon. Our book wasn't moving at all. But as the day progressed, it started to creep up the rankings. Suddenly, it appeared in the top 100 books in Small Business Marketing. And then it entered the top 100 in Entrepreneurship!

This is when the second great surprise occurred.

We started seeing our book, and more importantly, our *names*, on the same page with some of our favorite authors. I am a huge Andy Andrews fan. (If you have not read *The Traveler's Gift*, make that the next book you read after this one!) My book and my name shared the page with Andy Andrews! I have long admired the mission and marketing savvy of Dave Ramsey, the training of John Maxwell, the wisdom of

Napoleon Hill, and the research and insight of Malcolm Gladwell—and I was on the same page with all of these titans.

I was blown away. Never in my life would I have expected to be featured alongside authors such as these.

But it gets better!

Late in the day, our book started to creep up. Soon, we were right under these names. And then, we were *above* them! By the end of the day, our book was the #1 book in both of our categories and beat out books by Andrews, Ramsey, Maxwell, Gladwell, and even Napoleon Hill. I would have never imagined it, but my name was featured above many of my very favorite authors!

I am not sure I can explain how good this felt. I was shocked. And I was proud. I think I felt like I had won the lottery.

Here is where the most unexpected benefit occurred. As wonderful as I felt seeing my name associated with authors I respect so greatly, this feeling would only last so long. The surprise and joy faded, as they always do, no matter how great the experience. But something deeper remained.

Seeing my name next to (and above!) these authors left a lasting and unexpected impression in my mind. Glimpsing my book atop the list of bestsellers did too. Though I never planned this, I mentally started to take ownership of my accomplishment. I was an author! I was a *bestselling* author! And my book, if only for a moment, was selling faster than all of these accomplished authors.

This was a transformative moment in my business and personal life. And it was something for which I was completely unprepared. What I never expected was the impact of my book on my internal dialogue. My accomplishment affected my mental posture and confidence. These changes, in turn, affected how I approached prospects and clients. While I did not recognize any severe lack of confidence before publishing my book, the release and launch of *The Video Tractor Beam* gave me not just an external appearance of authority but also an internal gravitas that has since impacted many aspects of my life.

And this is only the beginning. As you will learn in the coming pages, a book has many powers. Some are subtle while others are overpowering. Some are predictable while others are wondrous and surprising. All of them together form something quite unique.

For this is *The Power of the Published.*

SECTION I
WHAT CAN A BOOK
DO FOR ME?

A few years ago, I found myself on a flight back from Virginia, where I had facilitated a mastermind event for a client. An elderly gentleman was sitting next to me. Though casually dressed, he wore a Tommy Bahama shirt and a watch that looked suspiciously like a Rolex. After the plane took off, we introduced ourselves, and I asked him what he did for a living.

It turns out, James lived in my hometown and was retired, having built and operated one of the most famous dining establishments in that city. Eventually, he sold this business. I was surprised to find myself sitting next to one of the real movers and shakers of my city but one I had never seen in the news.

"What do you do?" James asked.

"Well," I said, "I am a #1 bestselling author, and I…"

"Wait," James said, cutting me off. "Really?"

"Yes," I said, "a few years ago, I wrote a book called *The Video Tractor Beam*, and it became a #1 bestseller on Amazon."

The next words out of his mouth shocked me.

"You know, I don't think I have ever met an author in person."

I was surprised because I thought he would have met several authors before, sometime in his life. Here was a very affluent and connected individual, essentially a celebrity in a city of nearly half a million people. He was used to rubbing shoulders with the wealthiest and most accomplished people in town. And in all his years, in his various business dealings, social events, and travels, he had never once met an author.

That is, until he met me.

As you can imagine, the conversation that followed was transformed because of my status as an author. James did not see me as the average traveler or even the typical businessman. He saw me as an author and an expert.

That conversation is ingrained in my head because it taught me a valuable lesson. Authorship is rare. Even if you have met an author, I suspect you have not met many. While you have met with countless professionals of one kind or another, the likelihood that you have had substantial conversations with more than one author in your life is small.

Yet, there is more to authorship. Authors are not only rare; they are *revered*.

> At a time when we have lost more and more respect for celebrities, professional athletes, and politicians, we still treat authors with high esteem.

Perhaps you think "revere" is a bit too strong of a word. I don't. Just look around. Who is invited to speak on conference stages? Speakers who are, more often than not, authors. Who are the "experts" most often interviewed on local and national news? Authors. Who gets PBS specials? Authors. You cannot watch the morning shows or the evening news for more than a few minutes without being introduced to the author of this book or that.

Oddly enough, it is actually easier than ever to become an author. The availability of writing tools and self-publishing options has made authorship more accessible than ever, but we still hold authors in the highest regard. At a time when we have lost more and more respect for celebrities, professional athletes, and politicians, we still treat authors with high esteem.

And this is why authorship should matter to you.

You have the opportunity to become a member of an extremely exclusive club, one more limited than even the so-called "one percent." In fact, you could become part of the *one hundredth* of one percent. You can create a tool that will invigorate your business or brand. And you have the ability to leverage your status as an author to ignite your future.

For books are amazing and wondrous things. Let me show you why.

1

INSTANT AUTHORITY

"Publishing a book is one of the very best ways to establish your authority, grow your audience, and increase your business."

—MICHAEL HYATT, BESTSELLING AUTHOR

In the early '90s, I started a career as a vocational rehabilitation counselor (VRC). When I began, I was wet behind the ears and the "new kid on the block." Nonetheless, I was able to develop substantial market share in my region through very active and persistent marketing. I attended countless professional meetings. I went to conferences and seminars. And I tirelessly (and tediously) visited office after office to meet with potential referral sources, some of them three hours away from my home. Fortunately, I was young (26) and highly motivated. Eventually, over the next several years, more through brute force than anything, I was able to establish myself in my market to the point that I was one of the busiest VRCs in Central California.

I only wish I knew then what I know now!

If I had it to do over, I would have written a book about vocational rehabilitation as one of my very first steps. Somehow, I would have published that book, printed some copies, and started giving copies to every referral source I could find. That book would have rapidly helped me overcome my lack of experience and probably would have allowed me to cut my marketing in half! Of course, I didn't know anything about publishing at the time, and many of our modern publishing services and tools did not exist in the '90s. But had I found a way to write and publish a book then, I am convinced I would have compressed the hard-won results of three or four years of diligent marketing and networking into just one year—or less.

The Video Tractor Beam

Fast forward a bit. My lifelong friend John Riding and I founded a marketing company called The Solution Machine in 2007. Some changes to California's laws spelled the death of vocational rehabilitation for me, while John had recently sold his screenprinting and embroidery business and was looking to start something new. We both had extensive experience marketing ourselves, so we decided it was time put our knowledge to work in the marketing of others. For the next several years, we built up a clientele, performing a variety of marketing tasks: websites, printing, SMS marketing, follow-up systems, and lead capture. We did it all.

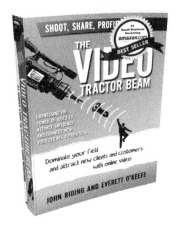

In 2012, we started to study video marketing and publishing. While John focused on the video side, I took a deep dive into publishing. In addition to finding out out what the web had to offer, I also learned many of the deep, dark secrets of the traditional publishing world from

"Dr. X," a publishing executive who anonymously created a brilliant and thorough exposé of his own industry so he would not be labeled a pariah.

Finally, after studying from some of the best in the self-publishing world, I told John it was time for us to test this knowledge by writing and launching a book of our own. After some discussion, we chose to write a book about video marketing since this was a service we had recently added to our business offerings. Essentially as a proof of concept, we wrote *The Video Tractor Beam: Dominate Your Field and Attract New Clients and Customers with Online Video.* We carried out the steps for a coordinated bestseller launch, and *The Video Tractor Beam* became a #1 bestseller on Amazon for a time.

> Though we had been doing video marketing for less than a year, we found we were now instant authorities on the subject.

Though we were now bestselling authors of a book about video marketing, we were still very new to the field. There were others in our town who had been making videos since the advent of the video camera, and others had been using videos in marketing for decades when we came along. But none of them (at least to my knowledge) had ever written a book!

But we did! We had a book, and it revolutionized our business. Though we had been doing video marketing for less than a year, we found we were now instant authorities on the subject. Our book conveyed expert status in the eyes of many people, and we started to get approached for video projects quite frequently. Even better, these prospects were already predisposed to hire us at generous rates because of the expert status implied by our status as authors on the subject. We were benefiting from the instant authority of a book.

David Frey: Pit Bull Secrets

David Frey is a consummate internet marketer and the author of *The Small Business Marketing Bible*. He is also a genius at spotting an opportunity and pursuing it. A few years back, he shared this story with me while we were waiting to present at a conference.

In the '90s, he wrote a small book, *Pit Bull Secrets*, and sold over 10,000 copies of the book.

"Everett, I didn't know a great deal about dogs, let alone pit bulls," he said. "But I noticed lots of people were searching for information, and no one was offering anything."

So, David did some research and wrote a little book. And then the phone rang.

"Hello," a man said, "is this David Frey, the author of *Pit Bull Secrets?*"

"Yes, sir. It is," David replied.

"Well, I am a reporter," the man said. "Did you hear about the lady who was mauled last night by her three pit bulls?"

> "I searched online for a pit bull expert, and your book came up. I want to interview *you*."

David told him yes. The reporter was looking for an expert to interview, so David referred him to an animal behaviorist in town that he knew.

"You don't understand," the reporter said. "I searched online for a pit bull expert, and your book came up. I want to interview *you*."

"It was crazy," David told me. "I just wrote this quick little book about pit bulls, and now, people were calling me a 'pit bull expert.' I ended up doing several interviews just because of this little book!"

David was an instant authority on the subject of pit bulls, whether he intended to be or not. His book had given him instant and recognizable credibility on the subject. Ironically, he had no desire to build a business around being the pit bull expert, but he did learn a valuable lesson.

"Books provide credibility," he said. "A book can instantly elevate you in the eyes of your prospects."

Armed with his experience, David started work on a larger book, and he was determined to make the most of it. He self-published *The Small Business Marketing Bible* because he knew the credibility and authority it would impart. He then used this book to build a thriving marketing and consulting business. David now uses the fruits of his book and his business for missions work throughout the world.

"Publishing a book gave me instant authority," he recently told me, "and that authority has allowed me to impact people in my business and in my missions."

The So-Called Instant Expert

I have just given you some examples of truly instant expertise, where people had limited experience in a field but gained expert status by publishing a book. But what about people who have been building their expertise all their lives?

You and I have both heard many stories of so-called "overnight sensations" in the music and film industries. Many considered The Beatles to be in this category because of their sudden, meteoric rise to fame. What many fail to note is the years they spent learning their craft and playing in clubs throughout Europe. Most people don't know that The Beatles played clubs in Hamburg, Germany, for more than two years, playing sometimes three or four sets a day and even living in the back rooms of the clubs where they played. They endured a brutal schedule and sometimes horrible living conditions, but this allowed them to perfect their craft. And *then*, after years of practice and performance, they became an overnight sensation.[1]

There are countless other stories of people who worked hard to develop their craft or acquire expertise and then benefitted from a sudden uptick in their fortunes. Musicians "get discovered" by music executives, athletes have a breakout moment that leads to a contract, and actors get the perfect role to propel them into the spotlight. Many times, it simply takes one opportunity to move from anonymity to fame and success.

More likely than not, you have worked very hard in your field. You have studied and practiced to make yourself qualified in what you do. Perhaps you have worked in your current field for years (or decades), or maybe you have recently taken your experience from a prior career and are now bringing it into the next venture. Either way, your business (or practice, or organization) is probably only one opportunity away from being an instant sensation.

David Martin is a very successful consultant to the CEOs and other executives of Fortune 50 companies, among others. He has done this work for decades. He recently told me of a funny event that occurred just two weeks after launching his book, *Free the Genius*.

> It simply takes one opportunity to move from anonymity to fame and success.

"I just got back from a college reunion, an event I attend every five years," he told me. "Since I had just published *Free the Genius*, I brought a case of books with me, and I was signing and handing out copies to everyone I could. While doing this, a woman I have known for 25 years approached me. She said, 'You know, I put on this event every year in the insurance industry. We are always looking for speakers, and it's a bonus if they have a book, so we can buy the book and have a book signing. Would you like to come to speak?' Now, she's known me for 25 years, and she has seen me every five years and has known what I do. But *only now that I have a book* did she consider inviting me to speak. The funny thing is I am the same guy I was 5, 10, 15 years ago, *but for her, I'm not*."

For David, his new book gave him instant credibility in a way that his successful years in business did not. While we can mourn the fact it took his friend 25 years to understand David's gifts, we can also recognize how powerful a book was in bringing about this change in her perception.

The truth is you may already be an expert in your field. Your training, skills, and experience may qualify you to wear that hat. But do your prospects and clients know it? Do they truly understand what an expert you are?

Of course, you can *tell* them what an expert you are. But that is likely to have limited impact. Many people may say, "If you have to tell me you are an expert, you probably are not an expert." In fact, we usually determine that someone is an expert when someone *else* calls them an expert. The newscaster or radio host introduces someone as an expert. An article in the paper or a magazine calls someone "the foremost authority." For your customers and prospects to accept you as an expert, you need someone (or something!) to declare your expert status.

A book does just that.

If your client or prospect sees your name on the cover of a book, it is as if someone handed them your book and said, "This author is an expert." After all, most people will assume that you must be an expert to have *written* a book, and you must *really* be an expert to have a book *published* on the topic! Most people do not know that it is easier than ever to self-publish a book. All they know is that you wrote a book, and that book has been published (self-published or otherwise).

From Anonymous to the World Stage

"Cindy," a coaching client of mine who wishes to remain anonymous, recently called me to let me know what her book had done for her.

"Writing and publishing my book," she said, "proved to be an incredibly powerful method to launch my new consulting business."

Cindy originally contacted me last year because she was planning to attend an international industry conference and wanted to make a big splash. She knew this conference could be a springboard for her business. She had been working on a book, so we discussed how she could use this book at the conference even though she was only going as an attendee. A short while later, she boarded her flight to the conference with several newly minted copies of her book in her bag.

"I gave copies of my book to select individuals who I felt could benefit from my services," she said. "These new acquaintances were visibly impressed. Some of them even read my book during the evening hours of the conference! As you can imagine, this allowed us to have meaningful discussions the next day."

So, what were the results?

She earned a generous consulting contract from one of the companies to whom she had given a book! Cindy tells me it has been a very productive relationship, and they are forecasting working together for a long time. Another recipient of her book asked her to become a contributing author for an upcoming college textbook.

"What an honor!" Cindy says. "I happily obliged, and the textbook is due to be published later this year."

And there is more. Cindy will be returning to the same conference this year, and this time, she will be going as a paid speaker! One of the contacts she made is sponsoring her to speak at the conference, where she will be able to showcase her expertise in front of prospects from around the world.

Consider this: In under a year, Cindy has gone from being an anonymous attendee at a large international conference to being a recognized expert in her field. Her book provided her with an excellent, paying client and placed her in a college textbook in her subject area. Don't let this slip by without considering the impact of this. With her contribution to the textbook, she is publishing alongside those people that academia considers to be experts! And now, her book has propelled her onto the world stage.

"A book positions you as an expert like nothing else," Cindy told me. And she should know.

Now, Cindy would be the first to admit that she had to work hard for her opportunities over the years, and she had to work even harder to develop her expertise in her industry. These things did not happen overnight. But her book allowed her to get noticed. It caused others to finally perceive her expertise and then caused them to regard her as an expert. This, in turn, led to paying clients, more publishing opportunities, a paid speaking engagement, and international authority.

> "A book positions you as an expert like nothing else."

Your book can do the same for you! It will provide you with instant authority. Whether you acquired your expertise over many decades or rather recently, your book is what will help others to see you as a recognized expert.

Great Power and Greater Responsibility

This is my sixth book, and Ignite Press (as of this writing) has been involved in more than 45 bestselling book launches. With what I know now about the power of a book, I am convinced that I could pick almost any field of study, write a book, and be regarded by many to be an expert in that field, all within 12 months. Maybe within six months. Or three.

What if I wanted to become a recognized expert on heart health? I could do some research, maybe interview some doctors, and then write a book about my findings. I could send copies of my book to radio and television stations or maybe hire a publicist to land some media appearances for me. And in a very short period of time, I could be seen as an expert on heart health. The fact that I lack a medical degree or any formal training will not matter in the eyes of many. What *will* matter is that I am the author of a book on heart health.

I am not saying I *should* do that. The world is full of enough snake oil salesmen and so-called experts who know next to nothing about the topics upon which they speak. I am simply saying that a book is powerful enough to establish expert status even where such expertise has not been acquired. It can also establish authority where expertise *has* been acquired but not yet recognized. Think about how much more powerful a book can be, therefore, when it is placed in the hands of someone who really has developed the needed experience and knowledge.

What is an expert anyway? While many unqualified people pretend to be experts, the reverse is also true. Many experts pretend *not* to be! I have met literally hundreds of people who were experts in their field but failed to acknowledge it. I don't want you to think that you can only write a book if you think you are one of the very top thinkers in your field. The truth is that you have knowledge and experience that you should share with others.

Erasmus famously said, "In the land of the blind, the one-eyed man is king." By themselves, your prospects lack the knowledge they need to make

You are the expert they need.

the best possible decision and therefore have the best possible outcome. While their "vision" is limited, you have both eyes wide open. You see and understand your field in a way that your prospects and clients likely never will. Whether or not you think you are *the* expert in your field, you possess expertise that is far beyond that of your clients and prospects, and they *need* your expertise. As my author/publisher friend Jim Lewis likes to say, "You owe it to them!"

In fact, you are probably the very expert who is most likely to help them. After all, if you don't, who will? If you fail to step up to the plate and hold yourself out as an expert to help people, who will they turn to? Will they turn to someone less skilled—or less scrupulous?

You are the expert they need, and your book will help them to see your expertise so you can get their attention and help them.

2

RARE AIR

A couple years ago, I was invited by my mother to speak to a women's group in my hometown. The group was comprised of retired professional women as well as the wives of many of the city's most successful businessmen.

At the start of my presentation, I asked the audience a few quick questions.

"How many of you," I asked, "have ever met a doctor?" Every hand in the room went up.

"All right," I said, "raise your hand if you have ever met an attorney before." Nearly every hand was raised again.

"How many of you have met a financial planner sometime in your life?" There was a sea of hands.

I could have gone on like this, naming profession after profession, but I decided to cut to the chase.

"How many of you have met an author before?" The women looked back and forth at each other. Slowly, three of them raised their hands.

I paused a bit and then asked the next question.

"How many of you have met a *#1 bestselling* author before?" The three women who had raised their hands before looked at each other. One of them (proudly) raised her hand.

That one was my mother.

Had I performed this exercise 10 years ago before I entered the world of publishing, this result might have surprised me. After all, I was speaking to the upper crust of a city of nearly half a million people. These women were the movers and shakers (or married to the movers and shakers) in my community. Many were part of the so-called "one percent" and moved in affluent circles. Nonetheless, only a few of them had met an author in person, and only my mother had met a #1 best-selling author.

But this shouldn't be surprising.

Consider this. There are currently approximately 1.1 million doctors of medicine in the United States.[2] The US population in 2017 was approximately 325.7 million. This means medical doctors comprise about 0.3% of the US population. In other words, about 1 of every 333 people is a medical doctor of one kind or another.

So what about authors? Some statistics indicate there are a total of 280,000 "authors, writers, and editors in the United States." But this number includes newspaper writers, bloggers, journal editors, and more. When we look at just "writers," we see something very different. The US Bureau of Labor Statistics says there were only 45,300 "writers and authors" in the US in 2017. Even this number is overblown, however, because it includes not just writers of books but also writers of scripts and advertisements. The number of book authors, therefore, is even smaller than 45,300.

> ....
>
> Authorship is a rare thing indeed.
>
> ....

If we use 45,300 as our number, that means only 0.0001% of the US population is an author! Whereas 1 of every 333 people is a medical doctor, only 1 of every 7,189 people has authored a book! (I apologize for repeatedly using exclamation marks, but this is a dramatic number.)

In reality, the Bureau of Labor Statistics is more than likely under-reporting the number of actual authors. The statistic is probably meant to describe the number of people *earning a living* as a writer. Looking at the number of books on Amazon alone, we know there are more than 45,300 authors in the US, but there are still very few when compared to doctors and other professions.

The truth is authorship is a rare thing indeed. Although pollsters have claimed that roughly 81% of the population hope to write a book someday, the reality is quite different. *Very* few people ever write a book. Those who have written a book have accomplished something exceptional.

But why does this matter? Who cares if very few people ever write a book? Really, what difference does this make to you?

Do this exercise with me. Describe in your head your geographical market. If you are a dentist or a chiropractor, your market might be a city or a part of a city. For a financial advisor or insurance agent, your geographical market might be a county or even a few counties. If you are a speaker or perhaps a consultant, your market may stretch across the states—or around the world.

Now, estimate how many people in your market do the same or something similar to you. I know many of you will say, "nobody does quite what I do." I get that. But just count up the number of people in your market that hold the same title or might somehow try to compete with you for customers. Depending on your profession and your market, this number could be pretty substantial.

There were more than 153,000 dentists in the US as of 2016, according to the Bureau of Labor Statistics. There were approximately 47,000 chiropractors and 501,000 licensed insurance agents in the US as of 2016. Whatever your profession or field, consider how many people are potentially in competition with you.

How many of them are authors?

Are *any* of them authors?

If so, how many of them are bestselling authors?

Unless you are a speaker or a high-level consultant, the odds are slim that your competitors are authors, let alone bestselling authors. They do not enjoy the "rare air" of being an author, and they do not enjoy the many advantages that come with this status.

The Air Most Rare: Bestseller Status

If authors are rare, bestselling authors are rarer still. Whether they are New York Times, USA Today, or Amazon bestsellers, these authors represent a very small subset of the author community. If you can accomplish a bestseller status with your book, you will have added a feather that you can wear in your cap for a lifetime.

A book that becomes a bestseller is not on the bestseller lists forever. The book may last for weeks on the New York Times or USA Today lists, or it may last for days on Amazon, but it will eventually fall off the bestseller lists.

Do you know what they call a bestselling book that is no longer on the bestsellers lists? A bestseller. Do you know what they call an author who no longer has a book on the bestsellers lists? A bestselling author. That's right. In reality, most of the books you have seen described as bestsellers are no longer on any bestseller list. And most bestselling authors no longer have a book on the bestsellers lists either.

Bestseller is an accomplishment that, once gained, cannot be lost. Once a bestseller, always a bestseller.

Let this thought sink in for a moment. If you write and publish a book and that book becomes a bestseller, you have the right to introduce yourself as a bestselling author for the rest of your life. And when people introduce you, they may

> If you write and publish a book and that book becomes a bestseller, you have the right to introduce yourself as a bestselling author for the rest of your life.

describe you in the same way. Add "bestselling author" to your bio on your website, and that can become part of how the host introduces you when you speak at an event.

Perhaps you think this is all well and good, but becoming a bestselling author is a "pie in the sky" notion. Let me tell you: It is not. Later in this book, I will tell you how you can become a bestselling author. As I write this, we have been involved in the launch of more than 45 books, and all of the books we have launched have become bestsellers, almost all *#1* bestsellers. As you are reading this, there are more than 40 authors breathing that rarest of air because of our assistance with their book launches. I don't share these numbers with you to brag; I share them to let you know that this rare air is available to you, too.

* * *

Want to discuss putting the power of the published to work for you? I would love to discuss your options with you personally. Please schedule a complimentary consultation at IgnitePress.us.

3

COMPETITION KILLER

"No single project has moved the needle more for my business than becoming an author."

—Frank A. Leyes, ChFC, Financial Advisor
and #1 bestselling author

I don't know in what profession you find yourself, but unless you are the sole provider in a highly specialized niche, you have competition. You may be in an industry with extreme competition or one where your competitors are distant and of little threat to you. Regardless, there are almost certainly other people and businesses who offer a service or product that is at least somewhat similar to yours.

But do they have a book?

Your competition may have a great product or service. They may have strong name recognition or a compelling value proposition. Your competitors may have greater market share, better connections, or a well-established history. They might even have a better product or a better price point.

But do they have a book?

Authorship is one of the most powerful tools available to your business. The single accomplishment of writing a book, especially when combined with a successful bestseller launch, can be leveraged over and over again in an incredible number of ways.

Consider this:

How many times are you given the opportunity to introduce yourself to others? Whether you trot out a well-rehearsed "elevator speech" or introduce yourself in a more casual way, what would be the impact if your introduction included these words?

"I am a bestselling author…"

How about these words?

"I am the author of a #1 bestselling book on [fill in your topic]."

Would these words change the equation at all?

The answer is a resounding yes! Being able to tell business prospects that you are the author of a book in your subject area is a huge advantage. The reality is that your prospects have probably met people who compete in your space, but they have probably never met someone who authored a book on the topic. And your accomplishment sets you head and shoulders above others. Unless you are in a business niche where authorship is almost required (and there are very few of these), the odds are that your competition does not have a book. As an author, you will automatically be considered to be an absolute authority in your niche. Whether your prospect reads your book or not, you will be regarded as an expert and probably *more* of an expert than any of your competition.

> All things being equal, most people will choose the author.

Place yourself in this situation. You have found yourself in need of a real estate attorney. You ask your friends and associates for recommendations, and two names keep floating to the top. In an effort to be thorough, you decide to interview them both to determine which attorney to hire. Both attorneys have professional-looking offices, dress in nice suits, speak clearly, and have good references. Both appear to be qualified.

But one of them hands you a copy of the book he wrote on real estate law.

Which attorney are you more likely to retain? Would you engage the attorney who appears to be fine in all other aspects, or would you go with the attorney who *literally wrote the book* on real estate law? If you are being honest with yourself, I am guessing you would probably choose the author.

All things being equal, most people will choose the author.

But what if things *aren't* equal?

What if the first attorney you interview is like those I described—professional office, nice clothes, good references, well-spoken? Maybe

·····························

All things being *unequal*, most people will still choose the author!

·····························

he even graduated from the Harvard School of Law. Let's just assume he is impressive in every way. And what if the second attorney is *less* impressive in some way. Maybe he doesn't dress quite as nice, or his office is in a bad part of town. Maybe he doesn't speak as clearly or even has some sort of speech impediment. And while the first real estate attorney graduated from an Ivy League school, the second attorney received his education at a local law school.

But he wrote a book on real estate law.

Which attorney would you choose? Is the choice clear? Even if you are influenced by the Ivy League education for attorney #1, does the book cause you to consider attorney #2?

All things being *unequal*, most people will still choose the author!

What's more, most people in this situation won't even read the attorney's book. And that doesn't matter. Just the *presence* of a book is a game changer and completely tilts the balance in favor of the attorney who wrote it.

This situation can apply to almost any service or industry. It is easy to see how a book can impact the businesses of attorneys of all kinds. But let's look at some other industries:

- Would you give greater consideration to a financial advisor who wrote a book on investing?
- If seeking an insurance agent, would you be impressed that your agent wrote a book about the various types of insurance?
- If considering a new dentist, might you choose the dentist who authored a book about the treatment of tooth decay?

These are some of the most obvious professions that can benefit from a book. Let's keep going.

- If you were in need of treatment for cancer, are you more likely to select a doctor who has written about the latest cancer research?
- Are you more likely to select the accountant who wrote a book on tax planning?
- Would you hire the computer security engineer who authored a book on cyber threats?
- How about an architect with a book about cutting-edge building techniques and materials?
- Or the solar company salesman who has written on energy conservation?

People want to hire the best person they can reasonably afford in a profession. A book gives people the impression (correct or otherwise!) that the author is the best, or at least among the best, in his or her profession. And it sets the author apart from all others.

4

THE ULTIMATE
STICK METHOD

Online marketers are constantly working on ways to help customers remain customers for as long as possible. In the world of paid membership sites, where people pay an ongoing fee to gain access to online training, marketers work very hard to make customers "stick." Since the cost of customer acquisition is often quite high, the key to profits is to somehow cause customers to remain paying customers. Therefore, marketers constantly seek the best "stick methods" to hang on to customers. They experiment with different price structures, annual vs. monthly fees, time-released content, extra incentives for extended memberships, and more. Savvy marketers know that people have an almost inbred need to keep looking for the next shiny object and that these same people often face buyer's remorse (consciously or subconsciously) at some point after the transaction.

Regret doesn't only apply to the world of online marketing.

Even after someone hires a professional, buyer's remorse and a desire to find the next shiny object can kick in. Over time, we all tend to second-guess our choices. Do you ever ask any of these questions?

- Is my accountant the best one for me?
- Would I get better service from another insurance agent?
- Will I make more money if I change financial advisors?
- Would I save money or have better results with a different doctor/therapist/lawyer/mechanic?

I am sure some of these questions ring a bell.

Your clients are probably asking the same questions about you! Though they once thought you were the best person for the job, they periodically wonder if they would be better served by your competition. Don't take this personally. It is a scientific phenomenon!

A 2013 survey by CreditDonkey.com revealed that more than 50% of people said they "often or sometimes feel guilty about purchases."[3] A 2017 article from *Psychology Today* says, "most of us experience unadulterated buyer's remorse from time to time."[4] Such buyer's remorse is entirely natural, as is questioning our own choices. Unfortunately, as time goes on, and especially after your client pays your bill a few times, these questions persist and grow. When a questioning client is confronted with an attractive offer from your competition, that client may leave.

Fortunately, you have available to you the ultimate "stick method": a book.

The *Psychology Today* article I quoted points out an important phenomenon. Scientists have determined that people's minds are constantly trying to reinforce the decisions they have made. Customers want to see themselves as good decision makers, so they constantly look for ways to justify their choices. This makes sense when you think about it. The mind is always second-guessing itself, wondering if it made the right decision. This puts the mind in a state of anxiety. To attempt to dispel this anxiety, the mind looks for ways to put this doubt to rest. So, it constantly looks for justification to verify the decision that was already made.

Here is where your book comes in. When clients second-guess themselves and look for justification for their choice, they need look no further than your book. Just seeing your book or hearing the title will remind them that you are an expert in your field. Should they read your book or just flip through it, they will find all the justification they need to verify their decision.

The increased authority that a book provides helps to prevent people from being drawn away by the competition. When they are tempted to leave you, something in the back of their minds says, "Heck, (your name here) wrote the book on this topic. He must know what he is doing. I doubt I will get anyone more qualified." Whether consciously or subconsciously, the book reinforces their selection of you because you are a published author. In their mind, the book makes you a verified expert in your profession and, therefore, the right choice. As a result, rather than being vulnerable to your competitors, your customers are likely to stand firm in their selection of you.

Ultimately, your book destroys competition because it makes you stand out above any competitors both in the acquisition of new clients and in the retention of existing clients. It is not only the best tool available to separate you from your competitors but also the best "stick method" available to keep your customers.

5

THE FORCE MULTIPLIER

"Give me a lever and a place to stand, and I will move the earth."

—Archimedes

In physics, a force multiplier is something that increases the effect of a force. Perhaps the most obvious example is a lever and fulcrum. Greek mathematician, philosopher, scientist, and engineer Archimedes claimed that all it took was a solid place to stand and a long enough lever, and he could move anything. If you have ever worked on cars, you have seen the same principle at work. The most stubborn nut will turn with ease if you have a wrench with a long enough handle.

Force multiplier means something in military circles, too, where a weapon or strategy can make a small number of soldiers far more effective. The Maxim gun is widely recognized as the first modern machine gun. Invented in 1884, it changed the nature of warfare. When British colonial forces were attacked during the Battle of the Shangani in Rhodesia (modern Zimbabwe), 700 soldiers equipped with five Maxim guns fought off 5,000 attackers. World War I is commonly called "the machine-gun war" because the presence of such guns rendered large, massed infantry attacks futile. A relatively small number of properly equipped soldiers could defeat such attacks and inflict horrible losses. The Maxim gun was a true force multiplier, literally multiplying the firepower of the men who wielded one.

You might consider this discussion of the Maxim gun a digression, but I have a point. You see, a machine gun multiplies the firepower of a soldier who wields it, and a book multiplies the power of the author who wrote it.

It is difficult for me to overstate the effect of having a book in your arsenal. As a society, there are few people we regard more highly than authors. We may respect doctors, pastors, teachers, and counselors, but these pale in comparison to authors. Maybe it is simply because we encounter authors far less frequently than we do these other people. I suspect it is really because of our attachment to celebrities. While our culture is awash with celebrities from television, music, and movies, you don't have to look too far back in history to discover a time when authors were the real celebrities. Before television and radio, writers were the famous ones.

> A book multiplies the power of the author who wrote it.

Consider these celebrities:

- William Shakespeare
- Jane Austen
- Mark Twain
- Charles Dickens
- Leo Tolstoy
- Homer
- Herman Melville
- Oscar Wilde
- Edgar Allan Poe
- Dante Alighieri

- Jules Verne
- Geoffrey Chaucer
- Charlotte Brontë
- The Apostle Paul
- Etc.

This is just a short list of people who became famous for their writing before the advent of radio and television. Many were the celebrities of their day, and we still regard them as such.

The celebrity status of authors continued into the 20th century, even after the appearance of radio and TV. Consider these names:

- Ernest Hemingway
- F. Scott Fitzgerald
- Virginia Woolf
- J. R. R. Tolkien
- William Faulkner
- Agatha Christie
- John Steinbeck
- George Orwell
- Dr. Seuss
- Isaac Asimov
- Etc.

The celebrity of authors continues to this day. Even with the added distractions of the internet and cable television, recent and present-day writers continue to enjoy celebrity. Just consider people like George R. R. Martin, Maya Angelou, Stephen King, Michael Crichton, Tom Clancy, J.K. Rowling, Nora Roberts, and Harper Lee, among countless others. Writers continue to enjoy elevated status.

Most of the writers I have mentioned are writers of fiction. When we move into non-fiction, we find many of the celebrities of the business world. Consider Dale Carnegie, Malcolm Gladwell, John Maxwell,

Dan Sullivan, Og Mandino, Stephen Covey, Napoleon Hill, Tony Robbins, Tim Ferriss, Elon Musk, Seth Godin, Jason Fried, and Perry Marshall, among others. At every turn, we are confronted with someone who has become a celebrity or has increased their celebrity status through writing.

I would also argue that writers are among our most revered celebrities. While the headlines are filled with the travails and moral failings of politicians, professional athletes, and radio/television stars, authors have largely been left unsullied by tabloid journalism. The controversies that hound many celebrities just don't seem to cloud the reputations of many of our writers.

The truth is that we revere authors in a way that is both difficult to define and also undeniable. When we read a book, there is a certain vulnerability that occurs. While you and I both are likely to adopt a very defensive position when being presented a sales pitch, we will often drop these defenses when reading a book.

There is power in a book.

Maybe it is the way the words on a page allow us to form our own images in our heads. The writer can share stories, examples, and information, and our mind takes this data and allows it to coalesce and solidify inside our minds. The space between the details leaves room for us to add our own ideas and interpretations. Soon, the story in our mind is as much our creation as it is the writer's. We have become *co-creators* with the author, and

> The relationship between the writer and the reader is a very intimate thing.

this allows us to subconsciously take ownership of the content. Brendon Burchard says, "People support what they create," and he is correct. When we have a hand in the creation of something, we want to see it succeed, and we are naturally biased toward it. When we read a book and co-create with the author, we are naturally disposed to believe the story we helped create. As a result, we are more accepting of what we read in a book than what is presented verbally or even visually.

We are also swayed by the long-form nature of a book. In this world of 30-second commercials and 5-second sound bites, the mere act of spending a few hours with a book opens our minds in a way that is hard to duplicate with any other media. The relationship between the writer and the reader is a very intimate thing. The writer can guide the reader through stories, facts, and opinions, moving the reader this way and that, spending literally hours together in the process. By the end of the book, having devoted so much time together, the reader feels connected to the writer in a way that just cannot occur within a normal business setting.

Ask yourself: How much time do you get to spend with your typical client or prospect? How much time do you have to convince prospects that they are in need of your services? If you are like most people, you may have only minutes (or just moments!) to sway a prospective customer. Not so with books. If you can put your book in the hands of clients and prospects, they may spend *hours* learning from you. Rather than being on guard while listening to a pitch in your office, your prospects will take you home with them. They will read your book while sitting on the couch and lounging around the pool. They will probably even take you to bed with them! Your clients and prospects will be listening to you, learning from you during their most relaxed and vulnerable moments.

Do you see the power of a book and why it is a force multiplier? It allows you to multiply the time you spend with each and every client. It allows you to multiply your effectiveness in communicating with your prospects. It also allows you to multiply the impact you have on the lives of your customers.

The Power of the Unread Book

By now, I hope you and I can agree upon the power of a book that is read by your client or prospect. The force-multiplying effects are ultimately undeniable and pervasive. But what about the book that is never read?

Face it. A large percentage of people who receive a copy of your book will never read it. This is a sad reality. While it is difficult to find statistics about the percentage of books purchased vs. those that are actually read, there is an easier (if anecdotal) way to measure this. Take a look at your own bookshelf. Whether at home or at work, my guess is you have a number of books that you purchased or were given to you that you intended to read someday but just have not gotten around to reading. Am I right? If you are like me, there are several books on your nightstand too, ones you set there in the hopes of actually reading some evening. (By the way, if you are one of those rare people who manages to read every book you buy, take my word for it. You are in the minority, and the majority of people buy many books with the best intentions but never get around to reading them.)

Now think of the books you own but have not read. Consider the authors. How do you feel about them? How do you regard them? Is your opinion of them somehow lessened because you have not yet read their book? Are you somehow holding in check any positive judgement on them? Or do you still consider them to be experts or authorities on their topics? My guess is you have already been swayed by each of these books and their authors in one way or another. In fact, the mere presence of these books on your bookshelf, desk, or nightstand continually reinforces the expert status of each of the authors. Every time you see the author's name on the cover, his or her celebrity status is reinforced. And yet, you haven't read the book.

It has long been my opinion that 95% of the people who will be influenced by your book will never read it. I have no studies to back up this claim. Yet, while the percentage may be slightly off, I know I am in the ballpark.

Consider this breakdown. Once you have written a book, you can classify the entire world in these nine categories:

1. People who do not know you have written a book
2. People who know you wrote a book but don't know anything more
3. People who have heard your book title but have never seen or read the book
4. People who have seen your book or an image of it but have never held it
5. People who have held your book but have never read it
6. People who have read the front and back cover and no more
7. People who have read only the cover and the table of contents
8. People who have read part of your book
9. People who have read all of your book

Of these nine categories, only one group will not be influenced at all by your book: those who do not even know you wrote one. All others will be influenced in one way or another.

Even people who have only learned that you wrote a book but are clueless as to its topic or title will be impressed because you joined the ranks of authors. They will know you took the time to do something about which they have always dreamed. And they will know you are among an elite few. Of the eight categories of people to be influenced by your book, these people will be influenced the least, but even they will be significantly impressed by your accomplishment.

As people learn more and more about your book, they will be further impacted. Those who hear your book title cannot help to begin to consider you an expert on the topic. Think about some of the radio interviews you have heard. You have probably heard countless guests who were also authors. Most talk radio shows introduce their guests in a manner like this: "Today, I have in the studio William W. Williamson, the author of *All Dried Up: Everything You Wanted to Learn about Dried Flower Arrangements but Were Afraid to Ask."*

Pause for a second. What is your opinion of William W. Williamson? You have not read his book. You only know that he has a book and that it professes to teach you something about dried flower arrangements. Without knowing anything more, most people will assume that 1) he has joined the elite ranks of authors and 2) he must be an expert at arranging dried flowers. You might also surmise 3) he has a sense of humor about his craft and his book will be entertaining based upon the witty title. Without having anything more than the title, you have been influenced by the book.

People who see your book cover will be influenced even more because they now get to see your name on the cover alongside the title and subtitle. This is a big deal. Provided that your cover looks professional and not like something created in MS Word, your status and credibility as an author and an authority are reinforced. Even if they never turn the book over, you will be forever cemented in their subconscious minds as an author and expert.

As people go further into your cover and content, they will be drawn closer to you and your influence. People who read the back cover and/or the table of contents will have a chance to understand the benefits you are promising to deliver through your book. If they stop there and go no further, they will also usually assume that your book fulfills these promises, provided, of course, that your claims don't appear to be too fantastic. Even then, many will assume that your

> **Even the *unread book* has great power!**

book fulfills its promises! Of the nine categories of people, only one will read your entire book. But all others who encounter your book will be influenced by its power one way or another. Even the *unread book* has great power!

I asked my good friend, Kathleen Meredith, about this strange power one day, and she explained it this way:

"When I have met or known the person who wrote the book that sits upon my shelf, even causally, I cannot help but smile," she said. "It's a reminder of my little brush with greatness. I believe I am not alone in feeling a little elevated by my association with the person whose name appears upon a book on my shelf. It creates a feeling of good-will—even if I have not read the book. When I've known the author well, it is like picking up with an old friend when I read their words and hear their voice come alive on the page."

As you can see, there is something mysterious about the power of a book, whether your client has read it or not!

Durable Marketing

Books are unique in other ways as well. One unique quality is their durability. I am not talking about how much of a beating they can take or whether they can survive a teething puppy (they can't!). I am talking about how long a book can endure as a marketing tool and how long a book can continue to work for you.

Most marketing is very short-lived. An ad in a daily newspaper is only useful as long as the prospect is looking at the page upon which it is printed. And when they throw away the paper, the ad is lost. A radio spot lasts only as long as the listener hears it unless something catchy or memorable gives it a more prolonged impact. Likewise, a social media post (paid or otherwise) is seen once and is then gone. Frankly, most advertising is fleeting in this fashion.

My friends in the advertising community will probably take me to task over that statement. Old-guard marketers will say that a person must have 5 to 12 encounters with a product before they will buy and that their ads provide these repeated encounters. They will probably also tell me that ads can have a subconscious impact and stay with a prospect longer than we might expect. I understand these things. But the truth remains; when I am sitting at my desk at work or my recliner at home, I am not thinking about the ads I encountered earlier in the day. Like most marketing efforts, these lack durability.

There are more durable marketing techniques. If you are reading this book at work, look across your desk. Do you have a pen or coffee mug with some company's logo on it? How about a mouse pad, cell phone holder, desk calendar, clock, or any other promotional item? I will wager that most of these items have crossed your desk. In fact, I will bet a free copy of my book that you have one of these items on your desk right now! (If I am wrong and have lost the bet, send your name and physical address to info@ignitepress.us. Tell my assistant that I owe you a book, and we will send one right out!)

If you are reading this book at home, the same bet stands. But start by looking at your refrigerator for a branded calendar or in your cupboard for some company's promotional mug. If that fails, look next to your phone for branded Post-it notes. These are all examples of more durable marketing.

These items are intended to provide repeated brand exposure and increase name recognition. The companies that provide them hope you will see that pen or mug one day and magically decide that you need their service right then and there. The sad truth is that, while these items are durable, they impart no credibility or authority. They are usually regarded as cheap trinkets, promotional swag that can be disregarded and disposed of at will.

Not so with books!

Books are the ultimate durable marketing product. They outlast any other marketing strategy I can think of because people don't throw them away! Look at your bookcase. Or explore that pile on top of your desk or credenza. Do you have any books there? If so, let me ask you a few questions. How long have you held onto these books? Are there some books that you are sure you won't ever read—but you are still hanging onto them? If so, how many times have you moved these books without throwing them away?

I am chuckling right now because I suspect you are at least a bit like me! I have several books on my bookshelf and on my desk that I will probably never read. But I have not brought myself to throw them away either. I consider them to have some inherent value that keeps me from "round filing" them. Maybe it is because I hold out some irrational hope that I will somehow read them someday. Because these are books, perhaps I know they must contain wisdom or other useful information. Regardless of the reason, I know I have not been able to get rid of them. What's more, I have another bookcase in my storage room with more books. I have gone so far as to get them out of my personal office and move them (multiple times, in fact!), but I still cannot throw them away.

Back to my friend, Kathleen. She says it this way:

"Our hesitance to discard books is embedded in our cultural consciousness. Books have been a vital part of our civilization and collective experience, and the burning and destruction of books is typically a very troubling occurrence."

If we have this deep-seated aversion to the destruction of books, why not put it work for you?

I was just explaining this to a client the other day when it hit me. Books have such longevity that many copies will outlast your clients—or you. Your book has the potential to be handed down from generation to generation. Can you say that about any other marketing product?

I am sorry for belaboring the point, but I think you understand. Books have this strange hold on most people to the point that they simply cannot discard them. Even if people finally discard them, the books hang around for months, years, or decades before they meet their fate! And where do books usually go to die? Is it the trash can? No! Most books are taken to used book stores or donated to libraries or charities! So even when we finally get rid of books, their lives are still not over. This is why I consider books to be the most durable of all marketing strategies.

Now for the best part about your book sitting on a shelf or desk. While promotional items like pens and mugs are durable, they are only suitable for brand exposure, while a book is a constant reminder of your expertise! Rather than shouting a brand name, a book continually (and calmly) speaks to your accomplishment as an author and authority in your subject area. Although someone may place your book on a shelf and never read it, that same person will encounter that book over and over again. Each time they do, that book cover (or even just the spine) will tell them what an expert you are. And you simply never know when your prospect will finally pick up that book and read it or simply give you a call.

So far, we have ignored another unique quality of books: people give them to friends, family members, and work associates! While people rarely pass along advertising or marketing materials to others (unless they are funny, of course), books are often handed from one person to another or given as gifts. Someone reads a book and finds it useful. They then loan or give the book to someone else in their office or family, and the cycle continues. The same book can touch multiple people's lives, and each life has a chance to encounter your message and be confronted with your expertise.

This is why a book is the ultimate durable marketing piece. A book really is the proverbial "gift that keeps on giving." While I know this may remind you of a joke or crass saying, this isn't far from the truth. There is nothing like a book to provide an enduring and impactful marketing message for years and decades to come.

The Influential Whisper

An author recently relayed a story to me that perfectly portrays the power of the published. In this particular case, however, it shows the power of the *soon-to-be*-published. You see, "Bill" is a financial advisor who experienced the power of a book before he had even officially released it. I spoke with Bill a week before his launch.

"I ordered some advance copies of my book because I wanted to give them to some key clients," Bill told me over the phone. "A week before my launch, I called up a new client and offered to bring a copy by his office. Instead, he asked me to bring the book by the house that evening."

"When I got to the house," Bill said, "my client and his wife had some wine waiting and congratulated me on my new book. We sat and talked about the book and their investments. Before I left that evening, they handed me six investment statements from competing companies and asked me to manage that money."

"I was blown away," Bill told me. "This couple had been clients for only three months. They had already entrusted me with a good sum of money, but now they wanted me to take on six other investment accounts!" Even over the phone, I could hear the smile in his voice.

"It had to have something to do with the book, Everett. It had to."

Bill hadn't even launched his book yet. All he had was a pre-release copy. Because he decided to share this with an existing client, that client was influenced by it to such an extent that it caused him to invest even more money with Bill.

As I hung up the phone, I realized why a book is so powerful.

A book is like a trusted friend who whispers advice in your ear. While you are considering your choices, he tells you which direction to go. Because you respect your friend so much, you give great credence to his advice. While you won't blindly follow his direction, you value his opinion above almost all others.

When you read a book, this trusted friend continually tells you that the author is wise and to be trusted. He tells you the author's statements are likely to be true. This "influential whisper" is continuously present, subtly affecting you as you read every page.

Do you doubt me? If so, let's test my statement in a couple ways.

First, think back through your time reading this book. Has the book been whispering to you about my credibility? Has this "influential whisper" moved you to see me as an authority on this topic? Has it caused you to see me as someone who is trustworthy? If not, then I have utterly failed. In that case, please let me know so I can revise (or unpublish!) this book.

If you are still in doubt, take the ultimate test. Buy or borrow a book by someone you completely distrust. Read a book by a politician you don't like or some celebrity you don't respect. I promise you, it will be a hard read. It will be a real struggle for you, but not for the reasons you think. You probably think reading such a book will be hard because you will disagree with many of the statements. But you encounter such statements all the time. In fact, you frequently see disagreeable headlines and hear such statements on the radio or the news. But encountering them in a book is harder! This is because you start to feel the conflict between the "influential whisperer" and what you know to be true. When you read disagreeable statements in a book, you are simultaneously revolted by what you read and *attracted* by the influential nature of the book.

In fact, the more you read a book by someone you mistrust, the more you may be swayed in their direction. You may start to feel some deeper connection with the author and encounter empathy where previously there was none. While you may not be converted to the author's argument, you will almost certainly gain a greater understanding of it while being drawn closer to the author and his or her story.

Stop and think about this for a minute.

If a book is powerful enough to foster greater empathy and connection with an author with whom you completely disagree, how much more powerful will a book be when it is written by an author with whom you have no such angst? And how incredibly powerful is a book if the author is someone you are predisposed to like?! In that circumstance, the book is no longer a soft, influential whisper but the strong voice of a trusted advisor.

* * *

In this chapter, I have listed only a few of the reasons that a book is a force multiplier for your business or organization. Whether we are talking about the durable nature of books, the unique influencing power of a book, or even the power of the *unread* book, it is easy to see the impact a book can have. A book multiplies the power of its author. Whether your goal is to increase the profits of your business or to amplify the message you have for the world, a book is definitely the most powerful tool you can choose.

6

THE PROFIT BUILDER

"If you want to increase revenue, write a book!"

—Jenn Foster, #1 International Bestselling Author

Yael Cohen, Get IEP Help

Yael Cohen is a special education advocate and the Founder of Get IEP Help. She assists parents of children with special needs to help ensure their children are getting the school services to which they are entitled, and often more. For almost 30 years, her hourly rates were stuck in the $75 to $100 an hour range.

"I didn't think that parents would or could afford to pay more," she told me.

So, for decade after decade, her rates hovered in the same range. She felt

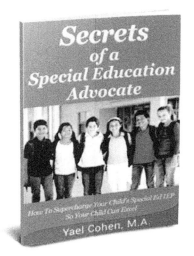

unable to charge more, so her rate remained more or less stagnant while her expenses and cost of living increased.

Yael attended the Aspen Mastermind Retreat for my Business Accelerator Group in October of 2014. While there, she was encouraged to finally raise her rates. Following the retreat, she did two things: She wrote a book and raised her rates. *Secrets of a Special Education Advocate: How to Supercharge Your Child's Special Ed IEP So Your Child Can Excel* was released in December of 2014 and became an instant bestseller in her field. And her rates? After nearly three decades of essentially stagnant fees, she increased them from $100 an hour to $150 an hour.

Did she lose clients over this? Almost none. Equipped with her excellent work record and her new book, Yael commanded the respect of her clients, and they were happy to pay her new rates. In the first year, despite a 50% increase in fees, only *one* person declined her services because of the change.

It gets even better. Yael recently told me that she has raised her fees yet again, this time from $150 to $200 an hour. She is finally getting paid a rate that is commensurate with the service she is providing, and her clients are happy to pay her.

Yael's ability to increase her rates is not due solely to her book. She provides an excellent service that fills an important need. But her book helped position Yael not just as an excellent advocate but as an expert in her field.

"Once I introduce myself at meetings as the #1 bestselling author of a book for parents of kids with learning challenges," she says, "no one really questions what I know. I didn't become any smarter after writing the book," she quips, "but people see me as more of an expert. And that makes a huge difference in what I can do for kids."

For Yael, a book helped facilitate an increase in her rates, and now, it helps her do her job more effectively. It gives her increased authority, which makes her work easier and also allows her to have greater impact for her clients. Who could ask for more?

By the way, you can find out more about Yael and her business at GetIEPHelp.com.

Andy Falco Jimenez, *Dog Sniff Evidence*

My good friend, Andy Falco Jimenez, was a K9 Officer in Southern California for many years. After retiring from law enforcement, he started a career as a dog trainer and as an expert witness in cases involving police and narcotics detection dogs. When I met him in 2013, his dog training career was well established, but his expert witness work was flagging. In fact, his finances were flagging too, and he had just received an eviction notice for his home.

Andy wrote and published *Dog Sniff Evidence* in December of 2013. While the content of the book teaches narcotics dog handlers how to preserve evidence for trial, Andy wrote it to help establish his own status as an expert in the field. He also wrote the book in such a way that it serves to educate attorneys working on cases involving narcotics detection dogs.

Following the launch of the book, which became a #1 bestseller in his niche, three things happened.

First, he was invited to speak at a legal conference at Caesars Palace. He found himself speaking in front of a large number of potential referral sources, and he made sure to provide a copy of his book to as many of them as possible.

Second, he started receiving cases from around the United States and even Canada. He soon found himself flying all over to testify in K9 cases.

Third, he nearly doubled his fees. Whereas Andy had struggled to bring in enough expert testimony work at his previous rates, he now had so much work that he was able to significantly increase his fees. Did he receive some pushback? Yes, he did—a bit. A couple of attorneys told him he was too expensive to retain. But far more gladly paid the fees because they were hiring the *expert of experts*, the man who literally wrote the book on detection dog evidence.

"It was the book," Andy later told me. "When I wrote the book and started putting it in people's hands, cases came out of the woodwork left and right! And that allowed me to raise my rates."

* * *

As a writer of a book, you will gain authority in your area of expertise, and most people will instantly consider you to be an expert in your field. Moreover, as we discussed in the chapter on competition, most people will regard you as one of the very foremost in your field. The best attorneys can charge more. The best marketers can charge more. The best [insert your title here] can charge more! Unless you are in a highly regulated industry where your fees are set for you, you can charge more.

When John Riding and I published *The Video Tractor Beam* in 2013, we experienced something similar. Although we really wrote the book as a proof of concept for rapidly writing and publishing books, the book had a very pleasant secondary effect. Local customers sought us out for video work, and they were willing to pay more for our work. After all, as authors (and #1 bestselling authors), we were regarded as experts in our space. Within a matter of months, we found ourselves able to charge twice our previous rates. In fact, later in the year, we closed our first five-figure deal. Was our work any better? No. Did we know substantially more? No. But we had a book, and that allowed us to expand our reach to more and better customers while increasing our rates.

Even in highly regulated industries, a book will almost certainly improve your profitability. Though regulations may prohibit you from increasing your rates, you can benefit in other ways. Your book may open new doors to you that were unavailable before. It may allow you access to a higher echelon of clientele. It will more than likely shorten your sales and conversion process so that prospects are converted into paying customers more quickly. Each one of these increases your revenue. If your book causes your clients to stay with you longer (see my chapter on books as a "stick strategy"), this will increase your revenue too, all without increasing fees!

When I started work as a vocational rehabilitation counselor in the '90s, our fees were limited by law to $65 an hour, and this is what VRCs charged. If I had a book at the time, I would have rapidly established more and better referral sources. And so, even working within the confines of the statutorily mandated $65 an hour rate, I would have increased my income through more billable business opportunities. In addition, working with the best referral sources would have allowed me to more rapidly create a solid reputation for myself. While I was ultimately able to accomplish all of these things, it took several years of exhausting (and costly) marketing. A book would have made the process so much easier.

> Would you be able to open up entirely new sources of business with your increased authority and access?

If you find yourself in an industry where your fees are regulated, consider the benefit of either more or *better* customers. Would a book help eliminate slow periods in your business and generate more stable, reliable income? Would your sales cycle be condensed, with people more readily moving from prospect to client? Would you be able to open up entirely new sources of business with your increased authority and access? Yes! A book can do all these things.

7

THE CREATOR OF THE PERFECT CLIENT

"Since you are creating clients anyway, why not create
the best clients?"

—Everett O'Keefe

Cynthia Freeman: This Is How I Work

Cynthia Freeman is a retired real estate agent in Southern California.
While she has moved on from the world of escrows and open houses,
she once was one of the most successful agents in the Los Angeles area.

And she didn't work weekends.

Let that sink in a bit. She was working in an industry that is known
for weekend work. The typical agent answers their phone for clients and
prospects nearly any time of the day or night, seven days a week. They
usually show houses or attempt to secure listings any time their clients

are available, and clients are most available on weekends. What's more, most sellers request that agents hold open houses; open houses are normally held on weekends.

But Cynthia developed a thriving business in one of the most saturated and competitive markets in the world—without working weekends.

How did she do it? She explained it to my mastermind group one day.

"I trained my clients," Cynthia told us while sitting around a fire in Yosemite. "In my first meeting with my clients, I told them, 'This is how I work. I work very hard for you during the week, and I make myself and my team available to you Monday through Friday. But I do not work weekends. That is time I need for myself in order that I may serve you better during the week. Should you call me on a weekend, please know that I will gladly call you first thing on Monday morning.'"

And she stuck to her own rules. When clients called on weekends, she called them back on Monday morning.

"Sometimes, they would get upset about it," she said, "but then I would just say this: 'Remember when we first met? I told you *this is how I work*. I work very hard for you during the week, but I do not work weekends so that I may work better for you during the week.'"

> There is great power in a phrase like, "This is how I work."

"I never had to remind a client of this more than once," Cynthia said. "They understood, and they quit calling me on weekends."

While there are several great lessons to be learned from Cynthia, I particularly love the way she trained her clients to be better clients. By doing so, she made her life more enjoyable, which helped her to avoid the burnout that is all too common in her profession.

And something else happened in the process. Because Cynthia did not fawn all over clients and make herself available 24/7, they saw her as the expert. They didn't see Cynthia as their slave but as their trusted advisor. Ultimately, her clients learned to respect her more because of the distance she created between them and her.

There is great power in a phrase like, "This is how I work."

What does this story have to do with a book?

Cynthia trained her clients how to be good clients. By telling them how she worked, she helped to sculpt their behavior and set the tone for their relationship with her. You can do the same thing (and much more) with a book.

I don't (normally) work on weekends. I used to. I used to work seven days a week and sometimes into those ridiculous hours that happen after midnight. No longer. There came a time where I decided that work happens during work hours, and I try to stick to that out of respect for my family and myself. I am not militant about this. I will sometimes use some evening hours for writing, but I do not take client calls or respond to client emails outside of regular work hours except in the case of some extraordinary event.

Stop. Look back at the prior paragraph. What did I do there? I just trained you, my reader, about how I work. I made it clear that I don't take calls or respond to client emails outside of normal work hours except in extreme circumstances. Should we work together in the future (and I hope we will), you will know that I protect my family and personal time but that I will be there to help you after hours in a real emergency. In giving you this information, I have started the process of helping us to work together in a better way, with proper boundaries. This will inevitably result in a better experience for us both.

Including statements like these in your book is one way to train your future clients to be better clients. There are more.

Ed Rush: You Have to Pay to Pay Attention

Let's say you are in an industry where you sometimes (or often!) encounter "tire kickers." You know who I am talking about: prospects who love to window shop rather than buy, people who want to tap your brain to get what free information they can acquire without any real intention of investing in your services. There is a way to head these people off at the pass!

My friend and mentor, Ed Rush, likes to say, "I won't work with people who are cheap on their way to success." Why does he say this? He says this so people who approach him will understand that they will have to make a significant investment to gain his services. Through this statement, he is prequalifying his prospects to weed out the ones who are unlikely to pay him what he is worth.

He also says that "people have to pay to pay attention." As a strategic advisor, Ed has had plenty of friends ask to take him to lunch to pick his brain. Being friends, he used to indulge these requests. Sadly, he quickly found that those friends who received free advice never acted on it. This was frustrating because he had consulting clients who paid him big money for the same advice he was giving his friends for free. And his friends would fail to do anything. Ed quickly learned that only those people who pay for the advice are likely to follow it.

"Now, if someone invites me to lunch to pick my brain," Ed says, "I tell them I am going to charge them for the lunch consultation! And I tell them they will thank me for it later."

Including stories like these in a book can have a profound effect on your reader. Quotes like, "I don't work with people who are cheap on their way to success" and "you have to pay to pay attention" tend to stick with your reader; they prepare the reader to pay for your services. Should you avail yourself of a complimentary book consultation with me, these quotes are likely to be floating around in your head. You will probably go out of your way to avoid being a "tire kicker" who just wants free information. What's more, you will also expect to make a substantial investment if you want my services.

Stories and quotes like these train your prospects to be better clients. They help establish your ground rules and set proper expectations. But there is another way to use your book to create better clients.

Pre-Educating Your Future Clients

One of the easiest ways to write a book is using the "FAQ/SAQ Method." I originally learned this method from Mike Koenigs, one of the most accomplished internet marketers in the world. I explain this method more fully toward the end of this book, but here it is in a nutshell.

The FAQ/SAQ Method is simply creating a book around the questions clients ask most often (FAQs) as well as the questions an intelligent client really *should* be asking (the SAQs or the should-have-asked questions). This is a fantastic way to write a book because you already answer most of these questions on a frequent basis, and you can probably dictate an answer to them without any significant preparation.

But it gets better. When you write a book that answers clients' most frequently asked questions, they stop wasting your time with them. If they read your book, they are less likely to take up your time with basic questions and may instead only ask you the questions that really make a difference (and perhaps a profit for you).

Let me explain with some examples.

If you were a financial advisor, would it be more profitable (for you and your client) to spend your time explaining what a mutual fund is or discussing which one would be best for the client? Likewise, would it be profitable to devote time to explain the "miracle" of compound interest or instead determine the best way to put it to work for your client?

Every industry has its FAQs. Whatever business you are in, there are some questions you answer day in and day out. A book written around the FAQs allows you to pre-educate your client before they ever sit down with you. It gives you a chance to explain (at length, if necessary) key concepts or definitions that are common to your industry. This helps minimize the time you have to devote to these often non-profitable discussions and lets you instead focus on topics that are ultimately more important and profitable for both you and your client.

Here are some examples of FAQs from a few industries along with alternate questions that are much more profitable to discuss:

INDUSTRY	FREQUENTLY ASKED QUESTION	QUESTION YOU WOULD RATHER ANSWER
Financial Advisor	What is a mutual fund?	Which mutual fund should I invest in?
	What is compound interest?	How can I take advantage of compound interest?
Insurance Agent	What is term life insurance?	What is the best type of life insurance for me?
	Who should I name as my beneficiary?	What is the best way for me to protect my loved ones?
Real Estate Agent	What is my home worth?	What steps can I take to increase the value of my home?
	What commission do you charge?	What is the value of the service you provide?
Chiropractor	What is chiropractic care?	Which type of chiropractic treatment is best for me?
	What's the difference between an M.D. and a D.C.?	Can you help me with…?

What are some of the FAQs for your business? And what are the questions that you would rather be answering?

If you are in an industry where you have a high volume of calls from existing clients and you find yourself buried in such calls, a book can help reduce this burden. For example, attorneys specializing in workers' compensation law often have to carry a very large client load to be successful. Because their fees are limited by statute, they must have more clients than in other areas of law, and many of these cases take years to resolve. Furthermore, their clients receive numerous legal notices that contain terms and concepts that are foreign to them. When faced with such confusion, clients often call their attorneys' offices for the most basic of questions, consuming a large portion of the office staff's time. The workers in these offices, and especially the attorneys, get buried answering frequently asked questions.

What if such an attorney had a book that explained the frequently asked questions in a way that is meaningful and clear? Would that cut down on calls and emails? Better yet, what if the attorney included a chapter entitled "When to Call Your Attorney"? Such a chapter could educate a client, instructing the client when a call to the attorney is important and when an unnecessary call can be avoided. This kind of chapter could also direct the client to other resources so the client can answer his or her own questions without any office involvement whatsoever!

> Since you are creating clients anyway, why not create the *best* clients?

What I love about this approach is that the same book you use to attract and convert clients can also make them *better* clients! You can make them better educated so they don't waste your time with unimportant questions. You can teach them how your office operates ("this is how I work") and when (and when not) to call. You can even teach them how to get the most out of your services.

This is a perfect mix. Your book can help set the proper expectations for your clients, and it can help your clients realize these expectations too. By making your clients better clients, you dramatically improve the chances they will be *satisfied* clients, and you will make your life more pleasant.

Since you are creating clients anyway, why not create the *best* clients?

A word of warning. You probably have stories and examples you use to answer these FAQs. That is common. If you place these in your book (and you should), just understand that you will at times bump into clients who have already read that story or example in your book. The first time it happens to you, you will feel uncomfortable, almost like someone revealed the punchline of a joke you are telling. Ultimately, you will learn to embrace this and realize you now have the freedom to simply skip that explanation and use your time more profitably. You may have to forgo using your favorite anecdote or quip if you have included it in your book too. But trust me on this. The extra time you gain is well worth it.

The Compliant Client

Savvy professionals understand that the relationship with their client is one of constant persuasion at one level or another. While most people focus on the persuasion required to move someone from prospect to client, persuasion doesn't stop there. Throughout the relationship, there continue to be key moments and decisions that require additional coaxing. A financial advisor may want to convince a client to make a specific investment. A doctor may

....

Books create compliant clients.

....

want a patient to accept a treatment recommendation. Whatever your field, there are times where you make a recommendation to your client in the hope that your client will go along with your advice.

I am sure you can tell me of a time where you had a client who balked at your every recommendation, a customer who asked for your advice but then refused to accept it. There are few things more frustrating. Whether you are a doctor, advisor, consultant, manager, director, or have any other title, it is always a challenge to manage a client who second-guesses your recommendations. In the legal world, this client is described as a non-compliant client. In medicine, this is the non-compliant patient. Whatever your field, you probably have a story you can share of a nightmare non-compliant customer!

I have good news for you. Actually, I have *great* news for you.

Books create compliant clients.

Throughout this book, I have discussed the many ways that books influence prospects and clients. Whether in the form of an influential whisper or the strong voice of a trusted advisor, books naturally move clients in the direction of compliance.

Should a customer read your book, he or she will be predisposed to accept your advice. Because of the elevated status and authority given to you as an author and because of the length of time your client spends with you while reading the book, your client is much more likely to follow your advice. While this doesn't mean that your clients will blindly follow your every recommendation (actually, they may!), you will find that clients who read your book will be extremely compliant.

Though this is true in general, it is even more true if the advice you give in person is coupled with the information in your book.

Let me give an example or two:

It has been my habit for some time to send new publishing clients a copy of my book *Books to Bucks: The Top 20 Ways to Make Money with Your Book (even if you haven't written it yet)*. I do this for several reasons. First, I want my authors to begin with the end in mind. If they start considering now how they might use the book we are publishing for them, then they will be better equipped to make maximum use of their book when we are done. Second, the book shows them some ways they can start using their book right now, even though their book is not yet published (or even written!). Third, I want my clients to be predisposed to accept my marketing recommendations down the road.

By the way, this third benefit was one I discovered by accident.

I was speaking with Chuck, a new publishing client. It was our second or third call, and I was explaining print-on-demand technology and why we would be setting his book up for this service. (As an aside, print-on-demand printing is a service that allows you to rapidly receive inexpensive copies of your book without having to order cases of your book or wait for overseas shipping. In essence, it allows you to order 1 or 500 copies of your book and have them in days at a cost of only a few dollars per copy.)

Now back to Chuck. I was explaining print-on-demand publishing. As soon as I brought it up, he said, "Oh yeah, I read that in your book. Let's do that!"

A few minutes later, I started to explain a strategy where you have Amazon send a gift-wrapped copy of your book to key contacts.

"Yes," Chuck said, "I read that in your book too, and I totally want to do that."

Without any serious explanation and without any convincing on my part, Chuck readily agreed with my recommendations. This was the first time I had encountered this but not the last.

A book is a powerful way to educate your clients and predispose them to accept your *general* advice. It is also an incredible way to prepare them to accept your *specific* advice on topics you cover in your book.

Take a look at your own situation. Are there topics or recommendations that you could include in your book to create a more compliant or profitable client? Are there frequently encountered concepts or barriers that could be overcome with a chapter in your book? Or, if there are concepts or challenges too complex to be overcome with a chapter, could you at least start the conversation so your client is well on the road to compliance by the time you meet?

If you sell insurance and favor a specific insurance product over another, for instance, how valuable would it be to explain the benefits of this product in your book and have a customer predisposed to purchase this product? If you are a surgical weight-loss doctor, how valuable would it be to explain the benefits of surgery in your book and have patients come to you already inclined to accept your recommendation? Better yet, how valuable would it be if you explained the dangers of non-compliance in the healing process so as to bring about a patient who better follows your post-surgical directions?

You can use a book to prepare clients for frequently encountered challenges that occur in relation to your product or service. Doing so can help prevent unnecessary stress for you and your customer. This makes for a more satisfied customer—and one less likely to leave you for your competition.

Are there aspects of your service that sometimes take a long time? Prepare your client by discussing them in your book. If you really want the lesson to stick, tell a story about a client who encountered such a delay and how everything worked out in the long run. If I were a workers' compensation attorney, where cases sometimes languish for years under a mountain of red tape, I would include a section in my book where I prepare the client for this, managing their expectations. If I were an orthodontist and got tired of patients undoing my great work because they refused to wear retainers, I would tell a story about a patient who did just that: wasted a ton of money and then came back years later and paid to have his teeth straightened again. If I refurbished classic cars and knew that unexpected complications often arise, I would spell these out in my book. If I were selling real estate and wanted to prepare my clients for the challenges caused by unsatisfactory appraisals, I would include a chapter about this and share some of the ways you deal with such challenges.

The possibilities really are endless, and they apply to nearly every industry.

If you are in the nonprofit world and create a book designed to increase donations, your book can cultivate donors and train them to be better ones too! If you prefer smaller but regular monthly contributions over larger, one-time contributions, use part of your book to explain why these types of contributions are more valuable. If you write a book designed for the recipients of your nonprofit service, use the book to prepare them for your service and perhaps cause them to be more responsive where needed. You will cultivate better recipients and probably improve your success rate at the same time.

Like I said at the start of this chapter: Since you are creating clients anyway, why not create the *best* clients?

What about your business or industry? Pause for a moment and consider how you can use a book to create better clients. Write down some challenges that frequently occur with your client base. Can you help your client be prepared for these challenges? Are there products or services that you commonly recommend? Can you use your book to predispose clients to embrace these products and services? Are there client behaviors that just drive you nuts? Can you head these behaviors off at the pass by discussing these situations in your book so that clients can be *better* clients?

Client Repellent

Most businesses work very hard to attract customers. They invest huge sums of money to find leads and try to convert them to customers. Savvy businesses, however, recognize that they need to attract the *right* customers. In fact, bringing in large numbers of the wrong customers can kill a business.

What would happen to a call center that is tasked with selling Viagra but is then provided a huge list of 20-year-old women to call? Will they get many sales? How much time and money will be wasted in the effort?

How about a BBQ restaurant that buys a marketing list filled (unbeknownst to them) with vegans? No matter how much the restaurant advertises to the list, no matter how many coupons they send, the results are likely to be abysmal.

Attracting the right clients is critical. Equally important is *repelling* the wrong clients.

A business needs to repel clients who are unable to pay, unlikely to be compliant, or who are unlikely to be satisfied. These types of clients are kryptonite to a business or organization. In fact, taking on these clients is at least twice as bad as not securing a client in the first place. Although they become a customer for a time, if they fail to pay or fail to do what you recommend, they waste your precious time and potentially became a negative referral for you. They also take up time you could otherwise devote to compliant and more profitable clients. Non-compliant customers are rarely satisfied with your services anyway. Such clients are, sadly enough, usually the most vocal in their complaints.

> Every business needs "client repellent."

Because of this, every business needs "client repellent."

Books are a fantastic way to repel the wrong kind of client or prospect. The long-form nature of books allows you to tell stories and use examples specifically designed to weed out the wrong people.

Let me share some examples:

Talking about the price of your services in your book is one way to push away people who are unlikely to make the proper investment in what you offer. I mentioned how Ed Rush says, "I don't work with people who are cheap on the way to success." Including statements like these in your book helps to repel people who want to work on a shoe-string budget.

I used some client repellent when I talked about Ed Rush and especially when I used phrases like "tire kickers." When I mentioned that you want to head people like this off at the pass, I made it clear that I don't want to waste time with people who are not ready to take action.

While I provide free book consultations, I don't want to meet with people unwilling or unable to invest in their futures.

The stories you share can push away the wrong people. So can the language. A casual tone will push away more formal people. Crass language will repel a prudish audience. I am not one to cuss a lot. If you want to repel clients like me, use foul language in your book. If you want to repel liberals, talk about liberals or their icons in a negative light. Want to repel conservatives? Do the opposite. There is great power in language!

Whatever you do, never give into the notion that your book is for everyone. In my world, a book for everyone is a book for no one. Your book must have a target market, and your language should always be attracting your target market while pushing away those outside this market.

Frank Leyes (financial advisor, speaker, and good friend) sprinkled quotes from Proverbs throughout *The Way of Wealth* for three reasons:

"Proverbs is full of financial wisdom," Frank told me while writing the book, "so it makes sense to quote it frequently. At the same time, I know this will resonate with a Christian or Jewish audience, and it will push away people who might be uncomfortable working with a Christian."

This isn't to say that Frank will only work with Christians and people of Jewish descent. Far from it. He is happy to work with people from any faith or background provided they meet his other client criteria (assets, perspectives about money, and such). Nonetheless, if someone is going to have a problem working with a Christian advisor, it makes perfect sense to nudge them away now rather than later in the sales process.

The end result? Frank has had many people come to him and rave about the religious influence in the book. Check out this review on Amazon. If you are in a hurry, skip to the last sentence.

By not attempting to write for everyone, Frank was able to establish a deep, heartfelt connection to the point that this reviewer is raving about him and telling all her friends! So, while Frank has been repelling some of the wrong clients, he has created brand ambassadors out of others! A true win-win.

I even learned of an author who created a book for a target market of only *five* people! He created a list of five CEOs with whom he wished to do business. He wrote the book with examples and language that he knew would resonate with these particular CEOs and published it! Then, he sent copies of the book to each person. And it worked! At the end of the day, he picked up new business that was worth far more than the investment he made in the book.

* * *

Books give you all the real estate you need (and more) to help prequalify prospects and train future clients. You have ample opportunity to tell stories and use language specifically designed to push away people who are unlikely to be satisfied with your services, and you can at the same time attract those who will be your ideal client. That is why I call books "The Creator of the Perfect Client."

8

THE EXPRESS LANE TO SPEAKING

Public speaking on stage has long been considered one of the most effective ways to influence society and share a message. Socrates and Aristotle espoused the power of speaking and taught "rhetoric" to their students. Now, 2,500 years later, speaking from a stage is still one of the most powerful ways to persuade crowds of people. Consider Abraham Lincoln's "Gettysburg Address" and Martin Luther King Jr.'s "I Have a Dream" speeches to behold the power of speaking in the public realm.

Nowadays, the vast majority of speakers are also authors. Pick up the program for any significant conference anywhere in the world, and you will see that most of the keynote speakers have books. In fact, even most speakers in breakout sessions will have books!

Event coordinators actively seek authors for speaking events. Why? It is simple. The last thing an event coordinator wants to do is place someone on the stage who tanks. If a speaker fails, then the event coordinator fails. But when a speaker has a book, there is the impression (correct or otherwise!) that this speaker must really know what he or she is speaking about. The book serves as "social proof" that this speaker is already successful and must therefore be an effective speaker. While we know this isn't always true, the book serves as an endorsement of the speaker. In fact, it may be the most powerful endorsement available.

> A book is an immutable monument rising over a sea of hype.

While a speaker can embellish their bio with various claims to make themselves look good, a book stands out as concrete proof of the speaker's credibility. A book is an immutable monument rising over a sea of hype. Its presence tells event coordinators and others evaluating speakers that they can rely on this speaker. And should the speaker fail to impress, the event coordinator can always say, "I thought he would be great. Heck, he has a book!"

Frank A. Leyes, *The Way of Wealth*

I mentioned Frank Leyes earlier. I met him at a conference in 2007. We had both recently lost our fathers, and we connected over our common pain—along with our faith.

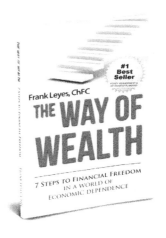

While Frank had managed his clients' finances for decades, he had also been developing a speaking career, speaking occasionally to other financial advisors at conferences across the nation. He also dreamed of writing a book. In fact, he told me in 2007 that he had been writing one for years!

He told me the same in 2008. And in 2009. And again in 2010.

In 2011, I decided to force the issue. I mocked up a cover for *The Way of Wealth* and sent it to him. I even went one step further. I had a single copy of the book printed and mailed to him. The inside was blank except for these words:

Frank!

Now we know what the outside of your book looks like. How about the inside?

Everett

In 2012, despite my polite nudge, Frank still had not completed his book. He continued to speak here and there, usually only once or twice a year as the opportunity arose. And he *talked* about writing his book. Ultimately, it took the publishing of my first book in 2013 to finally inspire him to finish writing his!

The Way of Wealth was published in August of 2013. It became a #1 bestseller, besting books by Dave Ramsey, Suze Orman, Robert Kiyosaki, and other icons of money management. Frank immediately started using the book in his wealth management practice. More importantly, he added the book to his bio on his speaking materials, and he started including a copy of the book whenever he reached out to event coordinators and others planning conferences for financial advisors.

The net result?

He received more offers to speak. He increased his fees, and he received still more offers. In fact, in the year following the launch of *The Way of Wealth*, Frank's speaking revenue increased 600%! While I am not at liberty to share precise dollar amounts, suffice it to say this made a significant difference in his business.

And the story doesn't end there. In 2017, Frank published *Shaping the Future*, a book written specifically for financial advisors. This led to his highest-paying speaking engagements yet. In 2018, because of his success with his books, he had the opportunity to sell from the stage for the first time. And on his first foray into selling this way, he offered a room full of advisors a $13,000 package and closed nearly half the room.

"None of this would have happened without a book," Frank told me afterward. "My books have given me the credibility to stand on any stage and address any audience. It is simply amazing."

Frank's story is not unique. If you study any of the most accomplished speakers, you will find that most of them either gained or increased their credibility and reach through books.

Brendon Burchard, *Life's Golden Ticket*

At present, Brendon Burchard is one of the most successful speakers in the area of high performance and personal development. In fact, he is recognized as "the world's leading high performance coach."[5]

He has appeared on public television, including Anderson Cooper, ABC World News, CBS News, Oprah and Friends, NPR stations, The Wall Street Journal TV, SUCCESS magazine, Inc.com, Forbes.com, FastCompany.com, and the Huffington Post.[6] All this to say, he's kind of a big deal.

So, do you know how he got started?

In 2008, Burchard wrote and published *Life's Golden Ticket* with the express intent of leveraging this book into speaking opportunities. In fact, he was able to parlay the credibility from this book into a relationship with Toyota and Junior Achievement. This partnership resulted in a series of big-top, circus-style events at Disney properties and launched Burchard's thriving speaking career.

Burchard continues to recognize the power of books. He has since written at least four more books. *The Millionaire Messenger* hit #1 on the New York Times list. *The Charge* reached #1 on the Wall Street Journal list, and *The Motivation Manifesto* was on the New York Times bestseller list for 32 weeks! *High Performance Habits* was released in 2017 and continues to cement his authority and expertise. Clearly, books have played a major role in Brendon Burchard's success.

Rachel Hollis, *Girl, Wash Your Face*

Rachel Hollis has parlayed years of hard work and the exposure of social media into something special. In 2018, buoyed by her social media following, she published *Girl, Wash Your Face*. It became a New York Times #1 bestseller and has garnered more than 10,000 reviews on Amazon (with a 4.6 average rating!). The last I heard, it had sold nearly a million copies.[7]

With the added exposure and authority brought to her by her book, she now speaks to packed *arenas*. She has become phenomenally successful, and many people now refer to her as the female Tony Robbins.

Hollis bristles at any suggestion that she was an overnight success. She makes it clear that she worked hard for 15 years before she got her big break. But there is no doubt that *Girl, Wash Your Face* dramatically increased her authority and reach. She understands the power of books and is continuing to put out more books (published and self-published) every year.

The Ultimate Speaking Catalyst

In the world of chemistry, a catalyst is "a substance that causes a chemical reaction to happen in a different way than it would happen without that catalyst."[8] Outside chemistry, a catalyst is something that brings about a change.

Books are the ultimate catalyst when it comes to speaking. They provide the added authority and exposure to help place you on stage. Whether your goal is to speak to a boardroom or an arena, the gravitas that comes from having authored a book is irreplaceable.

9

THE YOU-NEVER-KNOW FACTOR

So far, we have talked about how a book can predictably provide a number of benefits. We have discussed how a book can give you instant authority and provide expert status. We have discussed how a book can help you attract more prospects and convert them into customers more readily. We have talked about how books can help eliminate competition, cause customers to "stick" longer, allow you to increase your rates, and even train your clients to be better clients. All of these benefits are predictable.

There are many other benefits that are much harder to predict. Because of the unique nature of a book, events occur that are wonderful and surprising. I lump these events into what I call the you-never-know factor.

Drew and the MLM

"Drew," a member of my mastermind group, recently enrolled in a network marketing company (also known as a multi-level marketing company or "MLM") for the first time in his life. Drew is a true serial entrepreneur with multiple businesses. What's more, he understands the power of the published and has authored bestselling books to support his various businesses. Naturally, he decided to put authorship to work for himself in his latest endeavor.

Drew spent a few weeks studying his company's product, learning the science behind it, and formulating some frequently asked questions. Then, as he has done before, he quickly wrote a short and sweet book about the product, published it on Amazon, and carried out a best-seller launch.

Leveraging his book and other marketing techniques, Drew excelled in his company. He moved up in the organization at an unheard-of rate and soon had customers around the nation. In fact, after only a couple months, he was doing so well that he started to get calls from leaders in competing companies, all of whom wanted to recruit the bestselling author to their company. Though a rising star in his MLM, Drew began to sense some troubles in the company and ultimately accepted a lucrative offer from another MLM selling a similar product.

This is where it gets interesting.

Two weeks after beginning in this new MLM, Drew learned that the CEO of the new company would be speaking at a conference near his home. So, he grabbed a copy of his book and headed out to the conference with the plan to meet that CEO and put a copy of his book into that man's hands.

"I went up to him after he spoke and introduced myself," Drew told me. "I told him my name and held out my book for him to take. He took the book, looked at it, and did a double take."

"Wait," the CEO said, "you're the guy who wrote this book? I have this book on my desk at the office, and I just started reading it."

"You know, Everett," Drew said, "the CEO gave me his cell phone number right away and told me he wanted to have a meeting with me the next week. And I instantly went from just anybody to a superstar in his eyes."

You never know what a book will do for you. Because your book is available for sale throughout the world, you never know who will buy it or the impact it may have. Furthermore, because a book is durable, because people can pass it along from one person to the next, you never know how many people will read the same copy. And you never know how many people will recommend it to others or give it as a gift. You just never know.

And that is why I call this the you-never-know factor. There are countless ways that a book can impact your business, and many are impossible to predict. Drew went to the conference to give the CEO his book, but the CEO already had it (and had Drew on his radar as a result). By the way, the book has since helped Drew land several speaking opportunities around the nation!

Ron McLain: Healthy Marriage Coalition

On a Sunday morning a few weeks after publishing my video marketing book, a gentleman in my church approached me.

"I saw your book, Everett. I wonder if you can help me," he said.

Ron McLain is a skilled marriage counselor and the founder of the non-profit Healthy Marriage Coalition. He and his organization provide counseling, marriage classes, and retreats throughout California. Because he saw my book, he asked us to produce a significant marketing video for his next retreat—and the one after that. In fact, he soon told me he had been working on a book for the last several years and wondered if we could help him with that too. Thus, *The Resurrection Marriage* was born and became a #1 bestseller.

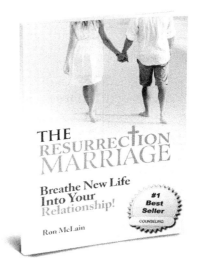

We have now had the opportunity to work with Ron and the Healthy Marriage Coalition on multiple occasions. In addition to publishing his book and creating marketing videos, we have filmed two conferences for him, created websites, and more.

And it started because he saw that I had published a book. The funny thing is that I really don't know if he ever read the book. I don't even know if he has a copy!

John Cote, Healthcare Elsewhere

John Cote is a retired marine pilot, airline pilot, and online marketing expert. You might think this is an unusual combination, and it is. But John became a recognized marketing expert because he did three things: he studied his topic, worked hard, and published a marketing book.

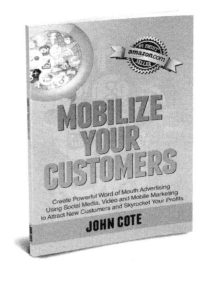

John wrote *Mobilize Your Customers*. At 120 pages, his book can hardly be considered a tome, and it is certainly not his legacy piece. Instead, the book is an intelligent, useful marketing piece meant to educate his readers and establish his credibility. The brevity of his book means his clients may actually read it and implement what they learn.

Mobilize Your Customers was published in 2012. In 2013, John received an unexpected call.

"I run a medical tourism conference," a woman on the phone said. "I googled 'word-of-mouth advertising,' and your book popped up. So, I bought it, we read it, and we want you to come speak at our event."

"Absolutely," John replied, "I would love to speak at your medical tourism conference! Uhm, but first, can you tell me what medical tourism *is*?"

The event organizer laughed and started to define medical tourism, the practice of traveling to another locale or country to seek medical care. Soon, she and John were discussing the terms of his presentation at the conference.

Shortly thereafter, John found himself as a featured speaker at this conference of 2,000 attendees, presenting to doctors and medical groups from 80 countries. John was very smart and brought a couple hundred copies of his book to give away; after his speech, people came up to him asking for his autograph, and many wanted to discuss hiring him.

> "So, I bought it, we read it, and we want you to come speak at our event."

John's notoriety lit a fire in his business.

You just never know, right? When John wrote and published his book, he had no expectation at all that it would lead to such an opportunity. And though he admits he knew next to nothing about medical tourism at the time, his book gave him an entry to speak at a medical tourism conference and gain customers in this field.

And it gets even better.

In his presentation, John discussed podcasts and how a podcast could help these medical practices increase their visibility.

"I challenged them to start a medical tourism podcast," John told me. "I had searched iTunes for podcasts on the subject, and there were zero. So, I told them they should market their clinics by starting a podcast focused on the successes of medical tourism."

Nobody took his advice. John watched the podcast lists on iTunes for many months, and no medical tourism podcast showed up. Not one to pass up a good opportunity, John started his own podcast where he interviewed patients who had traveled to foreign countries for treatment. Then, he had his episodes transcribed and put into a book.

In September 2014, John published and launched *Healthcare Elsewhere: Inspiring Medical Tourism Success Stories*. He did a bestseller launch, and it became an international #1 bestseller.

The following year, John was again asked to speak at the same conference. And this time, positioned with his podcast and new medical tourism book, he had appointments lined up with clinics wanting to engage his marketing services.

And the story isn't done yet.

At the end of his talk, John was approached by a gentleman from Central America. He and his business partners were in the process of creating an entire city dedicated to medical tourism, complete with clinics, hotels, and a new international airport. They had seen John's medical tourism book and watched him present on the topic, and they wanted to explore a business relationship.

The business group flew John and his wife to the city they were building and wined and dined them as they discussed the future of this venture. Initially, because of John's expertise, they wanted to engage his company for marketing services. Over time, as negotiations continued, they decided there was a better role for John; they asked him to join the board of directors and gave him an ownership stake in this huge venture!

You just never know where a book will take you. John did not expect his marketing book to place him on the stage at a medical tourism conference. When he wrote *Healthcare Elsewhere*, a book in a field in which he had no previous expertise, he had no idea where it would take him.

Books will do this! Their world-wide availability, combined with their durability and the authority they impart, provide strange and wonderful opportunities that simply cannot be predicted. This you-never-know factor is powerful, and it is a joy to behold.

10

WHAT INDUSTRIES CAN BENEFIT FROM A BOOK?

We have talked in some length about the many ways a book can benefit a business, and I have used some specific examples from various industries and professions. It seems appropriate to list a sampling of the many industries where a book can have significant impact. Keep in mind this is not an exhaustive list but simply a starting point. Perhaps you will find yourself on this list. If not, *should* you be on this list?

Industries and Professions that Can Benefit from a Book:

- Athletic trainers
- Attorneys
- Brokers
- Business executives
- Business owners
- Cardiologists
- CEOs
- Chiropractors

- Coaches
- Consultants
- Contractors
- Dentists
- Directors of nonprofit organizations
- Dog trainers
- Entrepreneurs
- Expert witnesses
- Fair directors
- Financial planners
- General practitioners
- General surgeons
- Gym owners
- Gynecologists
- Health and wellness experts
- Insurance professionals
- Marketers
- Oncologists
- Orthodontists
- Orthopedists
- Pastors
- Pediatricians
- Physical therapists
- Plastic surgeons
- Podiatrists
- Politicians
- Psychiatrists
- Psychologists
- Real estate agents
- Real estate brokers
- Sales professionals
- Salon owners
- Speakers

- Special education consultants
- Studio owners
- Thought leaders
- Veterinarians
- Weight loss physicians
- And on and on and on!

Can you think of a business or profession that should be on the list? If I am missing one, please email it to me! I am keeping a list and will refresh this book when I have gathered enough to merit the work! Please send your suggestions to info@ignitepress.us.

11

THE POWER WITHIN

The Most Unexpected Benefit

I started this book with the story of my first book. I shared the experience of first seeing my name on Amazon. Then, during our book launch, I saw my book ranked above my favorite business writers. It was more than just a surreal experience; it was also a transformative one.

While I like to talk about how a book gives you authority and helps you attract and close new and better clients, one of the most profound effects of a book will likely occur *in you*. What I never expected was the impact of my book on my internal dialogue. I had no idea that my accomplishment would affect my mental posture and confidence and, therefore, how I dealt with prospects and clients. While I expected the release and launch of *The Video Tractor Beam* would give me an external appearance of authority, I never expected it would provide an internal confidence that would affect so many aspects of my life.

This most unexpected benefit will surely vary from person to person, and I can tell you I have seen it over and over with my publishing clients. There is a transformation that comes over many of them as they move from the creation of the book through the launch of it. When I speak with them on the phone or meet with them by video, I can see the added energy and confidence that comes with accomplishing that which is challenging and rare.

Carole Herder is the owner of Cavallo Inc., an international supplier of equestrian equipment. She wrote *There Are No Horseshoes in Heaven* to highlight the challenges of traditional horseshoes and also to educate people on the benefits of the horse boots her company sells. While she says the book has had a significant impact on her business, she experienced this internal benefit too.

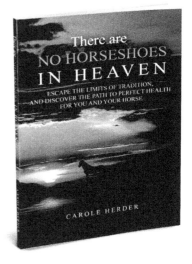

"My confidence has skyrocketed," she recently told me. "I so earnestly always wanted to be a published author!" Publishing her book gave her the tool she expected for her business, and it also increased her internal confidence and posture.

Don't overlook this benefit! Although I prefer to talk about tangible benefits (more clients, higher fees, better retention, etc.), the intangible benefits of authoring a book may be the most powerful for you. Should you write a book, call me a few months after your launch, and tell me what *you* think of the intangible outcomes that followed. I would really love to hear your experience.

12

THE MYTHICAL
SILVER BULLET

Marketers, like many business owners, would love to find a silver bullet to solve their marketing challenges. We want to find the perfect ad, the ideal tagline, or the ultimate way to bring in new customers. Sadly, silver bullets only work in *Dracula* movies. In the real world, there is no such thing. A tagline or phrase that works well for one type of prospect will not work for another. And what works great to attract new prospects does not necessarily help you convert them to become clients—or encourage them to *remain* clients.

This is completely natural. After all, the most effective marketing uses language, images, sounds, and even colors designed to target a very specific audience and move them to take an equally specific action. A plumber who wants to advertise emergency or weekend services must craft a message that speaks to those with water leaking on their floor right now. But a plumber who wants to attract remodel or new construction clients must use an entirely different message.

Companies also have to use different messages for customers in different stages. The message used to attract and convert a prospect might have a devastating effect when used repeatedly with existing clients. Financial advisors and insurance professionals often attract new clients by encouraging them to second-guess their current advisor or insurance representative. Frankly, this happens across many industries. Consider these slogans:

- Is your financial planner working for you?
- Are you paying too much for your insurance?
- What has your agent done for you lately?

While these phrases may work to attract new prospects, these are not the messages you want to send your existing clients! While you may be comfortable with the answers you would give your clients, you do not want them continually second-guessing your role and your effectiveness.

Marketing is never a one-size-fits-all business, and there are no one-size-fits-all solutions. Sadly, for this reason, there really are no silver bullets.

But books come close!

Of all the steps you might consider for your marketing, I would argue that authoring a book is the closest thing you have to a silver bullet.

Think of all the ways a book can help you. A book can:

- Provide instant authority by establishing you as an expert in your field
- Help qualify you for speaking and media opportunities
- Provide long-deserved recognition for your work in your industry
- Place you among an elite group of people who have authored a book
- Eliminate competition
- Provide the ultimate "stick method" to help customers *remain* customers
- Become a durable marketing tool to continually reinforce your credentials and expertise
- Provide valuable social proof that you know what you are talking about

- Serve as the "influential whisperer" that provides advice to your prospects and clients
- Allow you to increase your fees and provide justification for this increase
- Provide access to higher-value clients and more profitable opportunities
- Create perfect clients who are attuned to the way you work
- Attract the right clients and repel the wrong ones
- Predispose clients to accept your recommendations
- Increase confidence and internal posture

Besides authoring a book, can you think of any one thing that can bring about all of these outcomes? Can you think of something that provides even *half* of these benefits? If so, let me know! Seriously, send me an email at info@ignitepress.us if you have thought of something.

In almost 30 years of business, I have never encountered anything remotely as powerful as a book. When I published my first book, I was completely surprised by the varied and wonderful outcomes. In a very short period of time, the book provided me with new clients for higher-paying projects. It opened doors for opportunities that I would have never considered before. What's more, publishing my first book provided a change in my confidence and internal posture that I never imagined. This, in turn, has allowed me to work at a level previously unavailable to me. Because I took that first step into authorship, I have been paid to travel and speak internationally, developed a high-level paid mastermind group, and have aided publishing clients around the world. I have been amazed at the outcome.

And this is the recurring theme I hear from others who take the first steps on this journey. These are the words they use:

"It's just crazy!"

"Clients find me all the time—on Amazon!"

"I get emails from people all the time letting me know what a difference the book is making in their lives!"

"You should see the looks on peoples faces when they ask for a card and get a book instead. It is like magic!"

"My book has become one of the very best tools that I have."

"It's a crazy and wonderful journey."

If you would like to hear from these authors at greater length, visit the final pages, where I have included more of their stories in their own words.

SCHEDULE A COMPLIMENTARY BOOK CONSULTATION:

If you would like to schedule a complimentary book consultation, you may access our online calendar at IgnitePress.us.

SECTION II
HOW CAN I RAPIDLY
AUTHOR A BOOK?

You may have wondered why this section (and the subtitle of the book) refer to "rapidly" writing a book. Recall some stories so far, like Frank Leyes, who spent almost ten years formulating *The Way of Wealth*. Ron McLain worked on *The Resurrection Marriage* for several years before we helped him bring his book to fruition.

> ....
> The rapidly written book gets done; the slowly written book may not.
> ....

The truth is, most people think they don't have time to write a book! They think they will have to sequester themselves in a cabin in the woods for a few months to make this happen, and this simply isn't in the cards for most people. And it usually leads to frustration. While I have no objection to writing a book this way if you can pull it off, most people cannot. Even the ones who carve out huge blocks of time usually fail to bring the book to completion.

In my experience, the rapidly written book gets done; the slowly written book may not. Those people who attempt to write a book the traditional way often fall victim to distractions, time conflicts, and life events. As a result, what they thought they could create in a few months is still unfinished after a few *years*. I have seen it happen over and over again.

Therefore, I will devote this section of the book to the rapid creation of your manuscript. I want to set you on the path for success by giving you the tools to move quickly through this process. The speed of creation will not only dramatically increase the likelihood of success, it will also put your book to work for you in the very near future. With the training and guidance included here, there is no reason that you cannot have a book and see it launched to the world next quarter. So, think of it this way: Given the incredible power of the published, do you want to put a book to work for you in the next three to four months or in the next three to four *years*?

In addition to showing you how your book can be rapidly written, I will also show you how easy the process is. Yes, *easy*. Writing a book doesn't have to be hard. In fact, as you will learn, *writing* may not even be required!

Before I do that, we need to start with some fundamental and significant decisions.

13

WHAT KIND OF BOOK SHOULD I WRITE?

As you read this book, you may already know what book you want to write. You may have known for years! For you, the desire to write it and get it out to the world is growing and may have now reached a crescendo. But before you race off and start writing, listen to what I have to say. Take a few minutes to read this chapter. I may save you a great deal of time and money while helping you make more money for your business or organization in the process.

Many people who have desired to write a specific book for a long time desire to write the *wrong* book for their business. The book rumbling around in the backs of their minds is not necessarily the book they *need*.

First, if you have a legacy book in mind, something you want to pass along to your children and grandchildren, that is great. There is a place for this type of book. A legacy book can be a powerful testament to who you are while providing an opportunity for you to share poignant stories that have shaped you.

However, if you are considering a book to light a fire in your business or organization, you need to begin with the end in mind. Start by considering how you plan to use the book. Will you give it to prospects to influence them to do business with you? Do you plan to give it to existing clients to increase customer loyalty while encouraging them to engage with you at a higher level? Do you plan to use the book to position yourself as an expert to get speaking opportunities? Are you looking to make substantial royalties from your book?

By the way, if book royalties (the profit from book sales) are a substantial goal for your book, let me stop you. The average published book sells less than 250 copies a year, and a large number sell less than 500 copies in a *lifetime*. Is that shocking? Well, many sell less than 50 copies. If your book sales are average or below average, you are not likely to make substantial money from book sales. This is despite the fact that self-publishing your book provides a much higher royalty percentage than any other method.

Over the years, I have had the opportunity to look at the publishing agreements from several clients who went the traditional publishing route on previous books and then came to my company for publishing their next book. These agreements allowed royalties as low as 10%. Some of them included a provision to pay as much as 22% but only after 30,000 books were sold. By contrast, Amazon pays 60% royalties on paperbacks from the first copy, though after deducting printing costs. The royalty for Kindle books is up to 70%! But I still want to emphasize that royalties are often a poor reason for writing a book.

The reality is simple. You are not likely to make much from book sales. But you *are* likely to make money from your book in many other ways, as we discussed in the first section of this book. The increased authority and respect that comes with being published, combined with the ability to gather and convert new leads, keep existing customers, charge more, gain access to more valuable clients, etc., makes your book exponentially more valuable than any money from book sales. In fact, when you have your book in hand, it will probably pay off handsomely for you to give away as many books as possible, fully knowing that each book is your silver bullet and force multiplier!

Frankly, while you are unlikely to make any substantial money *on* your book, you can experience great rewards *through* your book!

So, let's get back to starting with the end in mind. Determine how you will use your book. Grab a pen if you like and start writing. Where and how will you leverage your book? What doors will your book open for you? Will it give you access to higher-value relationships? Will it place you on stage? Or on the local news or radio networks? Will you place the book in clients' hands? What do you hope they get out of the book? And how do you hope the book impacts them? What action do you wish them to take after reading (or even just seeing!) your book?

How you answer these questions will likely determine what kind of book you will write. The last question should particularly guide you. What action do you wish for readers to take? In other words, what do you want them to do after reading your book? Everything in your book should be crafted to support your desired outcome.

For example, before I started to even think about the content for this book, I determined the course of action I want the readers to take. In fact, I have two desired outcomes for this book. I wrote this book first to show readers how powerful publishing a book can be for them. Second, I wrote this book fully

> The desired course of action for your readers will determine your book.

knowing that some readers of the book, having been impressed with the power of publishing a book, will want a book for themselves. These people will then contact Ignite Press for assistance. In simple terms, I set out to write this book in the hope that readers would say, "Wow, I need a book, and I want Everett and Ignite Press to help me with it!"

The desired course of action for your readers will determine your book.

14

THE GROUND RULES FOR WRITING YOUR BOOK

"Don't get it right—get it WRITTEN!"

–LEE CHILD, NY TIMES BESTSELLING AUTHOR

The Video Tractor Beam

I mentioned before that I wrote my first book, *The Video Tractor Beam*, in 2013. Actually, that's not entirely correct. I never actually *wrote* the book.

Let me explain.

In February of that year, while driving back from a conference, I called my business partner from the car.

"John, let's write a book tomorrow."

Always one for an adventure, John said, "Sure. What are we writing about?"

"I don't know," I said. "But let's meet in the conference room at 10 a.m. and figure it out."

And we did. We sat down and spent roughly an hour planning out our very first book. Then we took an early lunch break. When we returned from lunch, we wrote the book. That day. In less than two hours.

But we didn't truly write the book; we *performed* it. With a microphone sitting on the conference table, we dictated the content of our book, one chapter at a time, until we felt we had covered the topic sufficiently.

....

We had created a professional-looking book without getting mired in a fruitless drive for perfection.

....

On the one hand, it wasn't a very good book. First, it was really only a brief, general overview of video marketing. It lacked any earth-shattering new strategy or information. Second, because *I* chose to edit it and perform the interior layout myself, it suffered in these areas as well.

On the other hand, it was a *phenomenal* book. John created a wonderful, engaging cover that could hold its own on any bookstore shelf. And that cover had our names on it. In a very brief period of time, we had created a professional-looking book without getting mired in a fruitless drive for perfection. Two weeks after completing the publishing process, we took the book through a bestseller launch, where it became the #1 bestselling small business marketing book on Amazon for a time.

I was now a #1 bestselling author.

But remember, I told you it wasn't a very good book. The content squeezed between the front and back covers was weak. There were (and are) much better books on the market. I am not proud of this fact, and I hope my subsequent books (including this one) are substantially better. Yet, remember this secret that many people fail to recognize:

95% of people influenced by a book *never read it.*

Though I cannot point you to a definitive source to back up this specific percentage, I instinctively know this to be true. First, when you write a book, people are influenced by the fact that you have become an author. Just writing a book is a huge (and rare) accomplishment all by itself, and people know this. Second, people are influenced when they see your name on a professionally designed cover. They are further impacted when they see your name alongside a catchy title and bene-fit-rich subtitle. They immediately (consciously or subconsciously) start to see you as an expert on the subject matter of the book. And when they turn the book over to see your headshot and bio on the back cover, the effect is complete. Your appearance there verifies your status. If you can add to this the accomplishment of bestselling author, the impact is even greater.

All of these things occur without the person even opening the book. The sad truth is that many people who buy your book may never read it. While reading habits vary, consider your own book collection at home or in your office. How many books have you bought with the best of intentions only to let them languish on your shelf? And how many have you started to read a book but never finished?

As an author, this thought may depress you a bit. Of course, you would like people to read and understand your message. But consider this. People will be influenced by your book, the cover, and your name on it *whether they read your book or not*. They will also largely assume that you are an expert in your subject area and that the contents of your book (which they may never read) will deliver on the promises made on the cover. Your book will have impact one way or another.

Let me demonstrate.

Shortly after our launch of *The Video Tractor Beam*, John was stand-ing in line at McDonald's when a man approached him. He must have known John from church or maybe from Facebook, though John did not recognize him specifically.

"Hey, aren't you kind of a big deal or something?" the man said.

"Why do you say that?" John asked.

"Well, I saw you wrote a book," the man said.

Here was a man who had never read our book. At most, he saw a social media post about the book launch. Nonetheless, he was influenced by the book.

Shortly thereafter, we were approached by a real estate agent who heard about our book launch. Though he never read our book, he saw our book cover on a Facebook post and knew we could help him build his business through video marketing.

Later that year, we were asked by an out-of-state marketing consultant to create a series of videos for his in-state client. And then, we were hired by a B2B business to create a DVD and video-sharing site about their product lines.

To our knowledge, none of these people ever read *The Video Tractor Beam*, but they were all influenced by it, so much so that they chose to invest significant sums of money to benefit from our apparent expertise.

So, in many ways, our very imperfect book was PERFECT! Though it was no piece of literature or tome of earth-shattering thought (far from it), it had the desired outcome. It positioned us as experts in video marketing, allowing us to attract new clients and increase our fees. What's more, we were able to bring our book to market quickly because we embraced this principle:

Perfection Is the Enemy

I first learned this principle from Frank Leyes. When we started working together, he asked if I understood that "done is better than perfect." I had to pause and consider this before I understood; it is better to complete a project than spend forever trying to make it perfect because no project will ever be perfect.

Later on, this notion was reinforced by Pam Hendrickson, one of my mentors, who taught "Perfection Is the Enemy." She tells her clients and audiences that striving for perfection in a product will delay and perhaps even prevent that product from coming to market. What's more, many of the things that you take the extra time to make perfect (or nearly so) are unnoticeable to your customer. Therefore, any delay while obsessing over unimportant details does nothing more than delay the benefit to your clients while simultaneously impacting your earnings in a negative way. Therefore, "perfection is the enemy."

Ultimately, this notion takes many forms. Voltaire is credited with saying, "The best is the enemy of the good," while Confucius said, "Better a diamond with a flaw than a pebble without."

When it comes to books, there is no such thing as a book without errors. And there is no such thing as a book that cannot be improved upon in some way. I guarantee that, no matter how much you choose to obsess about your book, you will find additional ways to improve your book as soon as it is launched! But if you wait until it is per-

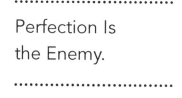

Perfection Is the Enemy.

fect or even *just right*, your book will never move beyond the manu-script stage.

This is why New York Times bestselling author Lee Child says, "Don't get it right—get it WRITTEN!" Don't beat yourself up in a futile attempt for perfection. Instead, get your book done quickly so you put it to work now. Wouldn't you rather have a *good enough* book working for you now than have a masterpiece that never gets done?

The 80% Approach

Sometime back, Dan Sullivan, the founder of Strategic Coach, released a short book called *The 80% Approach*. At only 40 pages long, it's diffi-cult to call this a book. However, the impact of it is quite significant. In this brief little book, he explains what he calls "the 80% Approach." This is not to be confused with the 80/20 Principle or the so-called Pareto Principle, which indicates that roughly 80% of your sales may come from 20% of your clients or any other permutation of 80% as compared to 20%. In *The 80% Approach,* Dan Sullivan indicates that no matter how much preparation we put into a project, our first iteration of that project is likely to be an 80% project, meaning that it is roughly 80% good (or, arguably, 20% bad).

Whether he's writing a book, creating a video, or designing some other project, he argues that his first pass at that project will never result in anything better than an 80% good project regardless of the level of his preparation. Furthermore, he goes on to say that his next pass at that project to improve it will never make it more than roughly 80% better. Now, if you do the math here, an 80% project that is now made 80% better is now a 96% project. He argues that most projects never require more than two passes or maybe three passes at most. He points out every subsequent effort to improve the project has diminishing returns, and the third and fourth passes will probably make only minuscule improvements, improvements that only the creator of the project is likely to even notice. Therefore, he argues, it is imperative for people to complete their first 80% of a project in a rapid fashion because preparing over and over to do it will never make it better than that first 80% anyway. He also argues that perfection is the enemy when it comes to creating anything. No project will ever be perfect, no matter how many times you attempt to make it so. Therefore, why not create the project right away and accept that it will never be perfect?

There really are two lessons to be learned here. The first is that preparation, while valuable, does have a point of diminishing returns. There comes a time where any additional preparation that you do before executing on a project is really just wasted time. Now, don't mistake me. Preparation is absolutely critical, and even a few minutes of preparation will likely save hours of frustration, while an hour of preparation will likely save days of frustration in the future. So, don't skip the preparation, but don't agonize over the preparation to the point that you fail to execute. If you know that the project will ultimately never be perfect, then why not execute an imperfect project early instead of failing to execute a project at all?

The second lesson to be learned from *The 80% Approach* is that your efforts initially will only create a product that is roughly 80% good and that, ultimately, nobody else can help you on that product until you have gotten your 80% done. Once you have completed your first 80%, other people can come in and add to your product and add their 80% to now make it a 96% project.

There is no place where this is more true than in the area of publishing. You have within your brain the collected knowledge and experience of a lifetime, and you want to pour that out through a book to help other people. Until you are able to get your 80% out of your head and into an editable, readable format, nobody else can help you with your book. That's why it's important for you to sit down and get this content out. Once you have it out of your head and into a Word or Google document, other people can come in and improve it. They can rewrite it if that's necessary. They add to it or edit it. They can augment your work with pictures or research. But until you've gotten the content out of your head and created your "80% good" project, there's really very little anyone else can do to help you.

There is a third lesson of value in *The 80% Approach*. Dan Sullivan emphasizes the point of diminishing returns where each successive pass or effort through a product improves the product in ultimately only marginal ways. This is especially true when it comes to editing and proofreading. Having a qualified editor go through your work to clean it up and make it look professional is invaluable. There really is nothing worse than putting out a book that is full of grammatical errors and typos. However, there is no such thing as a perfect book. Every book, no matter how many times it has been edited, reviewed, or proofread, has mistakes in it.

Let me share a story. Several years ago, we were working with an excellent client who had written his book and was in the process of proofreading it. Although the book had gone through a couple rounds of editing, my client found several errors that he felt the editor should have caught. Indeed, we always hope the editor will catch every mistake.

Unfortunately, this is never the case. In this particular case, my client was unhappy with the editor and felt like mistakes such as these would impugn upon his integrity if people were to find these errors in his book. As a result, I had a conversation with the editor and ultimately changed the project to another editor. By the time we were done, the client was very pleased with the book. Even then, the book had some small errors that had gotten by the new editor. If you think about it, these errors got past not one but two editors, a proofreader, and the client too!

I wish I knew then what I know now. I would have directed him to a book that was almost certainly in his library, *The Greatest Salesman in the World* by Og Mandino. If you happen to have that book, or at least the edition that I have, it says that there are 14 million copies in print, and yet, you cannot get two pages into the introduction without finding two grammatical errors. Let me emphasize. There are over 14 million copies of this particular book in print (actually, many more by now!), yet these errors exist. Does anyone question the integrity of Og Mandino on the basis of these typos? Do these errors take away from his work or his impact?

While we prefer not to have errors and do everything within our reasonable power to eliminate errors in a book, there will always be some. The truth is that we should embrace the imperfections, understand that they will occur, and move on anyway. If we continue to try to create a perfect product, we will spend all of our time in the failing effort to make our first product perfect and never get to the second, third, or fourth ones. This is true in books, and it is true in other areas of our lives as well. This isn't intended to be an excuse for shoddy work. It is intended to be something that should free you up. If you can stop stressing about perfection and simply create a product that is professional enough to accomplish the goals that you have, then you will move forward and have success. If you stress or obsess about making the perfect product, you will fail to bring that product to market, and you will fail to bring the next ones to market too. In the end, a desire to adhere to perfection will fail you, and it will fail your clients too.

* * *

Equipped with an understanding of the 80% Approach and knowing that "perfection is the enemy," let's look at three ways to rapidly create a book and put it to work for you or your organization. These methods are no excuse for shoddy work. They are simply ways to get the hard part of writing done quickly so that you and your clients can benefit from your book in the coming months.

15

RAPID BOOK METHOD #1

The Repurposed Book

Online marketers are masters at repurposing content. Rather than create content for one platform and then create it again for another, they create once and then reuse the same content over and over on various platforms. An extreme example looks like this:

A content creator shoots a live video on Facebook or Instagram. The recorded video is placed on Youtube and on the creator's website. The audio of the video is made into a podcast. The video is transcribed. The transcription is made into a blog post, Facebook post, and an article on LinkedIn. A link to the article is placed on Twitter.

In this example, one live video is made into eight different posts and formats. The content creator only has to be involved in the first part of the process. The rest can be accomplished by assistants or technology.

If you happen to have any appropriate content available, this could potentially be repurposed into a book. Existing blog posts, articles, podcasts, and training videos are all great sources, as are recordings of speeches or presentations. Transcripts can be a quick and easy foundation for a book. Leveraging your existing content is by far the fastest way to create your book.

David Martin, *Free the Genius*

Back in Chapter 1, I mentioned David, a high-end business consultant who coaches Fortune 50 business executives. He really knows his stuff. Until recently, he was also a frustrated author. You see, he had been wanting to write a book for more than 15 years, but he never could carve out the time to sit down and write one. On the other hand, he had been blogging for years! Over time, he had written a substantial collection of blog posts on a variety of

subjects that were all useful to business people in one way or another.

A few months ago, David was introduced to me by Scott Mann, one of my favorite clients. David had seen what we had done for Scott's projects and wondered if we could help him. At our first meeting, I could tell that David desperately wanted to finally get a book out, but he was also overwhelmed at the prospect of writing a book while managing his existing business.

"There's this blog I have been writing for years," he told me. "What would it look like if we packaged my blog entries into a book? Could we make that happen?"

"Absolutely," I said. "In fact, that is one of my favorite ways to write a book!"

Within minutes, we were formulating how he could arrange his blog posts into short chapters. He was excited because he saw a way forward. He was proud of his blog posts, and assembling them into a book was a perfect solution. David sorted his blogs into six logical categories, and these categories became sections in the book. His favorite blog posts became 44 short chapters. By the time were done with editing and layout, *Free the Genius* was a 180-page book and accompanying Kindle.

Free the Genius launched in March of 2019 and became a #1 bestseller in the United States and Canada. David couldn't be happier.

"I talked for fifteen years about writing a book," he told me. "I met you less than six months ago, and now, I have a bestselling book."

Creating a book from his blog was a freeing experience for David. It allowed him to get over the hurdle of creating his content, something that had blocked him for more than a decade. He told me that what really kept him from moving forward in the years before we met was the fear that writing a book and publishing it would be a "constant slog." We have since opened his eyes! In fact, getting one book done has opened the floodgates for him.

"Writing *Free the Genius* took the monkey off my back," he said recently. "Now I have at least two more books that I'm ready to write!" Many books on the market today are simply collections of blog posts that have been repurposed into a book. *Julie and Julia* by Julie Powell came about this way, as have *Rework* by Jason Fried, *The Dip* by Seth Godin, and many others.

> The very fastest way to create a book is to reuse content you already have.

If you have existing content available as blog posts, website content, videos, articles, and podcasts, repurposing this material can be a fantastic and rapid way to create a book. The very fastest way to create a book is to reuse what you already have. While this option is not available to everyone, you may have a collection of blog posts, social media entries, or articles you have written in the past. You might have training videos and recordings from prior speeches. If you do, these can be an excellent source of content for your book.

But what if you don't have a bunch of content waiting to be repurposed into a book? What if you need to start from scratch? Never fear; there are other ways of easily and rapidly writing a book!

16

RAPID BOOK METHOD #2

The FAQ/SAQ Book

Let me give credit where credit is due. I first learned this model from Mike Koenigs, and I am forever grateful to share this with you!

One of the easiest types of books to write follows a simple model by addressing the most common questions that arise in your industry. I discussed this briefly in Chapter 7, but we can give it more attention and detail here.

The FAQ/SAQ-style book is built around the most frequently asked questions (FAQs) in your business and then moves on to address questions clients *should* be asking ("Should Ask Questions" or SAQs). Together, the answers to these questions can form the bulk of your book.

Do this brief exercise with me:

Write down 10 questions that your customers or prospects ask you all the time. Take a few minutes if needed, and jot these down on a piece of paper. If you are having trouble coming up with these, simply think back to the last initial meeting or phone call you had with a new client or prospect. What were their concerns? What were their objections? Did they have questions about your product or certain features of it? Were their questions about price? Or timelines? What about legal questions?

Every industry has their own FAQs. If you work in insurance, you may encounter questions about the differences between term insurance and whole life. If you are a financial advisor, your FAQs may deal with the amount of money needed to retire or the future solvency of Social Security. A chiropractor may encounter questions like, "Can adjustments injure me?" or "Can I avoid surgery with chiropractic care?"

What are the frequently asked questions in your industry or profession? Write them down. In fact, write down as many as you can think of. I have sat in convention halls where people were tasked to write as many as possible in only three minutes. One time, someone came up with 48!

Now, turn your attention to the SAQs, the questions people *should* be asking. These questions can be more challenging, but they allow you to show your expertise. These are the questions people might ask if they really understood what was important. They often reflect a deeper knowledge of your topic.

For instance, a question frequently asked of financial planners is, "What are your fees?" But the question a prospect should really be asking is, "What is the value of an advisor?" Fees must always be viewed against the backdrop of benefits. Fees really mean nothing unless you also know what value the advisor can provide for the fees. The cheapest advisor is worthless if they provide no value. And the most expensive advisor in the world could be a downright bargain if the benefits provided by this advisor outweigh the costs.

In publishing, people often want to know how many pages they should write for their book. But the question that should be asked is how many *words* they should write. Given the variations in formats and fonts, along with the use of illustrations or stock imagery, page counts can vary dramatically. By the way, we normally recommend 25,000 to 40,000 words. Depending on formatting, this can create a book of 120 to 160 pages, long enough to feel substantial in the hand but short enough to be read on a cross-country flight!

In a car dealership, one of the most common questions is, "What is the monthly payment for this car?" People ultimately want to know if they can afford the monthly commitment. But savvy buyers know that they should instead be asking, "What is my cost out the door?" And if they are engaging in car payments, they should be asking, "What will this car cost me over the life of the loan?" They should also be asking about the total cost of ownership, including gas, insurance, maintenance, depreciation, and replacement. These are the "should ask questions."

What are the SAQs for your business? What questions should people be asking? If you are struggling to come up with SAQs, you have a couple options. First, look at each of your FAQs and consider if there is a corollary question like in the examples above. You might need to write down more FAQs to find the SAQs.

This is also a place where you can put the internet to work for you. My friend Bruce "the Book Guy" Jones suggests doing Google searches on your topic for inspiration. You can also use the auto-suggest function at Google. Type in your subject, and see what Google suggests for you.

Here is a really great tool. Go to AnswerThePublic.com, and type your subject in the search box. The site scours a database of Google and Bing searches and provides a huge list of questions being asked about your topic. This is a treasure trove of information!

If you are still having trouble finding the SAQs, don't fret. Just write down more FAQs and use them instead.

Ultimately, you should write down a total of 20 or so questions between your FAQs and SAQs. In my experience, most people can write down 30 to 40 such questions, sometimes in only a few minutes. Take some extra time to do this if needed. If possible, poll others in your industry to get their input. They will probably help you think of things you have missed.

Now, look at your list of questions. I expect that if I were to ask you any of these questions, you would be able to answer them off the top of your head. In fact, you have probably answered some of these questions so frequently that you have an oft-repeated, canned response. Great! Because in the FAQ/SAQ model, each question forms the basis for a chapter.

If you have 20 questions, you have 20 chapters. You now have the option to write out your answers to the questions (the old but still completely acceptable way of doing things), or you can dictate or speak your answers (the much faster method). Either way, if you can write 1,000 words or so on each question, you now have 20,000 words for your book. If you add an introduction, conclusion, and bio section, you will probably have 25,000 words. If you find that your answers are less than 1,000 words, simply add more questions! And if that isn't working for you, add brief stories associated with the questions.

Some people are more comfortable writing the answers to the questions the traditional way using a word processing program or even pen and paper. If that's what you prefer, great. If you go this route, though, you have to set yourself a daily goal. Remember how to eat an elephant, one bite at a time. Determine what you can bite off on a daily basis. I have found that I can easily write about 500 words each time I sit down. But if I am inspired and am attacking a fun or juicy topic, I can blast through 1,000 words. Breaking an FAQ/SAQ book into chunks, I can easily write this type of book in under 30 days.

Let me encourage you, however, to perform your book instead! It is so much faster. Using any number of recording tools, you may be able to plow through your FAQs and SAQs in lightning fashion. If you speak your answers, you have several advantages. First, your answer will tend to be conversational rather than analytical and boring. The conversational style may appeal to your audience better than a more formal voice. Second, you probably won't overthink your answer. If you simply start speaking as if you were answering someone's question, you will rapidly get the information out of your head and onto paper, where it can now be organized, tweaked and edited.

This method is so simple! This is the very method we used to write

The Video Tractor Beam back in 2013. We sat down for a short period of time to write out questions people frequently ask about video marketing. Then, we wrote down questions people should instead be asking.

Here is the chapter list for *The Video Tractor Beam*:

- Introduction
- Video Marketing
- How can video marketing help my business?
- Why does video marketing work?
- Do I have to make expensive videos?
- Do I have to be funny to make marketing videos?
- Do I have to be good-looking to make marketing videos?
- What equipment do I need to make marketing videos?
- Are marketing videos expensive?
- What is the best place to put marketing videos?
- What content should I put in my marketing videos?
- How long should a marketing video be?
- How often should I post marketing videos?
- How long does it take for a video to become available?
- How do I post marketing videos online?
- Do people really watch marketing videos?
- What is the best way to post videos online?
- Can I just post videos to YouTube?
- What format is best for online marketing videos?
- Do I have to have a website for video marketing?
- Is video marketing right for my business?
- Are there other ways to use online video?
- Do I have to do all this by myself?

This is nothing more than the list of questions we came up with while sitting around the conference table.

Next, we set up a microphone and laptop computer and started dictating the answers to the questions. We then sent the audio files to a transcriptionist, and we received the transcript a few days later. Voilà! We had our manuscript!

Guess what. Life is even easier for you. Technology has rapidly advanced, and there are now a number of excellent recording and transcription apps on your smartphone. The Rev.com app (iPhone and Android) allows you to dictate directly into your phone. Then, with a push of a button, your files are sent to a remote transcriptionist who transcribes your recordings! Files are technically supposed to be transcribed within 24 hours. In reality, most files are transcribed in under one hour because they are doled out among multiple transcriptionists. The price at present is $1 per minute.

Then, there is the Otter.ai app (iPhone and Android). This accomplishes the same essential tasks but uses artificial intelligence (A.I.) to transcribe your files. As such, the turnaround is essentially instantaneous. Better yet, the basic plan on the app is free to use. The downside is that it is not nearly as accurate as a human transcriptionist, at least for now! Expect the accuracy of A.I. transcription to improve rapidly over the coming years.

Keep in mind that *how* you get the words on the page is not important. The important part is that you do so one way or another. Once the words have gone from your head onto paper (or into a computer document), then you have something that can be now edited and organized either by yourself or others. Remember the 80% Approach above. Getting the content from your head and into a useable format accomplishes the first 80%. The next 80% can be provided by you, another writer, or an editor.

Using this FAQ/SAQ model can allow you to outline a book literally in a matter of minutes. If you choose to dictate your content, you can essentially write your entire book in an afternoon! There is no need to seclude yourself in a cabin in the woods for a month or two (though you are still welcome to do that if you want!). You don't need to disrupt your normal business life either. Instead, you can rapidly create your core content and be prepared for the publishing process!

17

RAPID BOOK METHOD #3

The Interview Book

In Chapter 15, we discussed repurposing content to create a book. One of the categories of repurposed content was audio or video content from podcasts and interviews. Well, what if you don't happen to have this content available to you?

Create it!

Many professional ghostwriters interview their subjects at length to gather the information needed for a book. Great ghostwriters are masters at this. But you do not have to employ an expensive ghostwriter to create a book from scratch. One very effective and rapid method is the interview method.

Books to Bucks

In 2015, I received a call from bestselling author Jenn Foster. She was in the process of building her publishing company and wanted to collaborate on a book about ways that authors could make money with books. We discussed the desired outcome (remember to always begin with the end in mind!), and then we talked about how we would write it. We were both very busy at the time publishing books for our separate clients. We also knew that the likelihood of us dividing up chapters and actually writing the content was, in a word, slim.

Jenn then suggested we create the content by interviewing each other. And that is precisely what we did. We set four appointments for conference calls where we could talk and also easily record the conversation. We used Skype at the time, but you can easily accomplish this now with Zoom, BlueJeans, and various apps on your smartphone. We used our first appointment to plan the book. Since we wanted to educate authors about ways to make money with their books, the FAQ/SAQ model didn't seem appropriate. Instead, we brainstormed and came up with 20 ways to make money with a book. We then created a list of questions that would help lead us into a discussion of each of these 20 ways.

Over the next three calls, each less than an hour long, we took turns interviewing each other. We had a free-form discussion of each of our 20 methods. Then, we sent the recordings to be transcribed. With a few conference calls and some money paid to a transcriptionist, we had created 95% of the material for our book!

We still had some work to do. Transcripts of this nature are rarely ready for prime time. Most people don't prefer to read transcripts in their natural state. What's more, we didn't want the book to read like a transcribed interview. Therefore, we both went through the manuscript and did our best to turn the transcript into a manuscript. In the process, we wrote an introduction and conclusion, added our bios, and otherwise prepared it for editing and layout. These tasks that we took on could just have easily been handled by a writer if we chose to hire one. And if you create a book from an interview, remember that you can hand off the lion's share of the remaining work once you have provided the content. This example is one way you can create your 80% and allow the next person to come in and add another 80%.

Jenn and I created the core content for *Books to Bucks* in less than 10 hours of cumulative work. Had we done the interviews and then employed a writer to clean things up, I am guessing we could have spent less than five hours. Keep in mind that the content was already in our heads for the most part. We did not attempt to fill the book with research, quotes, and stories. The addition of these components would have added many hours to a project. And in the case of *Books to Bucks*, much of that content would have been superfluous.

The interview method is a rapid and very accessible way to create a book manuscript. With the availability of smartphone apps like Rev. com and Otter.ai, creating a book in this way requires no special equipment or expensive software.

While Jenn and I chose to interview each other, this method can be used with just one author as well. All you need to do is create a list of questions that will lead you into a discussion of your content and then hand this list to someone to ask you the questions. A bit of advice: It is very valuable to be interviewed by someone who understands your content and goals. Such an interviewer will be able to ask relevant follow-on questions that will allow you to flesh out your content more fully. He or she may also help you avoid ambiguous statements that might be misinterpreted. A knowledgeable interviewer may add related content, just as Jenn and I did for each other in *Books to Bucks*.

* * *

Whether you create a book from repurposed content, use the FAQ/SAQ model, or use the interview method, keep your eye on the end result: putting a book to work for your business or organization in the near term. And remember that you are not, in this case, writing your memoirs or your legacy piece. You are writing a marketing and authority piece that will impact you and your company like no other! So, keep in mind that "perfection is the enemy" and that "done" truly is "better than perfect." Keep these things in mind, and you will have great success.

But What If You Really Want to Sit Down and Write?

What if you want to write your book the traditional way? That is never a problem as long as you can see yourself crossing the finish line. Some people love to write. If I am interested in a topic (like this one!), then I enjoy sitting down at my laptop to bring my ideas to life. For this book, I chose to use a combination of performing content and typing it the old-fashioned way. And that worked for me and my content. Ultimately, I have provided three rapid alternatives to the traditional method of book writing, but I have worked with plenty of clients who preferred to write rather than repurpose or perform their book. All methods are valid if, and only if, they result in a completed book.

18

WHAT'S NEXT?

Completing your manuscript is a huge accomplishment. While there is still a great deal of work ahead to turn the manuscript into a published book, most of that work can be done by others. For the busy business professional, getting to this stage means the finish line is finally in sight. And the book that you thought you might write "someday" is now ready to be published.

This chapter is intended to give you a basic overview of some of the remaining steps in the publishing process. Quite honestly, very few authors are qualified to perform these tasks themselves. There is value in knowing your personal strengths, and there is value in professional assistance. I have a B.A. in Literature and Composition, and I completed 40 graduate-level units in Creative Writing. I also taught English at two colleges.

And—I do not edit my own books (anymore, anyway!).

With the exception of my very first book, every book I have written and every book we have published has been edited by a professional editor. Editing is, like all of the steps below, best handled by the professionals. If you attempt to edit, layout your own book, or create your own book cover, you will likely be disappointed. Why put in the work to create a great manuscript to ruin it with poor execution in the final stages?

But you should have a general understanding of these steps so you are comfortable as your book proceeds toward the finish line. By the way, with the exception of content editing, we take care of all of these steps for our publishing clients. But even then, a basic understanding is very valuable.

What steps remain? Let's walk through them briefly.

Content Editing

Actuaries are among the most powerful and influential voices inside of the insurance industry. Their work underlies some of the most far-reaching and critical strategies for managing risk among these financial giants. Their research determines the pricing upon which products are designed. Their work helps craft the products that the marketing department promotes and the underwriting department manages—the products that investment portfolios are all designed to support. ~~Don't let the stereotype of coke bottle glasses and geeks in cubicles distract you from the essential message echoing from this group.~~ These actuaries are planning for a reality that you and I also need to acknowledge: Longevity is changing the game.

The most recent innovations in insurance products have an underlying assumption you must recognize. Before an insurance company can assume a risk, it must quantify that risk. The starting point for that evaluation is longevity. Believe it or not, many of these insurance products are now designed to work around policyholders that live to age 105! You read that right: 105! If the insurance companies are renegotiating around the vastly changing landscape of longevity, so must you.

Content editing

Content editors are tasked with reading your content and providing you with feedback to make your book better. They don't concern themselves with grammar and punctuation. Instead, the content editor often takes a big-picture look at your book to make sure it flows logically without leaving gaps or loose ends. In a fiction book, the content editor may watch for consistency among people and place names or offer input about issues like character development, pacing, plot turns, and continuity. In a nonfiction book, the content editor might tell you that you need to move a chapter from point A to point B or ask you to delete your content in Chapter 3 but expound more on the concepts you cover in Chapter 8.

Good content editors are very expensive and rightly so. They take on the responsibility of making sure that you fulfill on the promises you make at the start of your book. They have to have a strong enough mastery of your book content to understand what you are trying to accomplish and then exert influence to move your book toward that goal. A passing familiarity with your content just won't cut it.

Quite frankly, many self-published authors forgo this step. To save money and time, I often recommend authors find someone in their network to review their book and provide content suggestions. Many people have an associate in their office or another professional in their network that has enough expertise in their subject to provide useful feedback. This can be very valuable. Getting another set of eyes on your book is always a good idea. Every writer has blind spots, and new eyes can help fill these blind spots. What's more, writers tend to fall in love with their work. Every baby is beautiful to its mother, and this can be true when it comes to books too! Have someone you know and trust read your book. Carefully listen and consider his or her feedback.

A note about feedback: When considering feedback, always consider the source. Since this is your book, you get the final say about your content, and you should not feel obligated to take all the advice you receive. No matter how well-intentioned your reviewer may be, he or she may be wrong! Consider advice through this lens: does your reviewer understand your target market? Does he or she understand your desired outcome? Does your reviewer have some understanding of the strategy you are employing with your book? If the answers to these questions are all yes, then give the recommendations great weight. Even then, this is your book, and you must feel great about it when you place it in a prospect's or client's hands. If making a suggested change will erode your pride in the book or cause it to fall short of your desired outcomes, feel free to ignore the advice that has been offered.

Copy Editing

Whether you have em-
ployed a professional content editor or have instead
utilized someone you know
to function as a reviewer of
your content, your manu-
script is now likely in need
of a copy editor. Unless you
are a flawless writer (and I
have yet to meet one!), you

Copy editing

will need a professional copy editor to go through your work and correct grammar and punctuation. While you may find an alternative to a
professional *content* editor, there really is no substitution for an experienced *copy* editor. I strongly recommend you have your book reviewed
by someone who does this type of editing for a living. Although your
aunt Martha may be a retired school teacher, your book is too important
to leave to her expertise. Trust me. Have a professional edit your book.

Some copy editors also perform fact-checking roles, but never assume this. In fact, most copy editors will not choose to be responsible
for your content at all. They will correct your punctuation and grammar, suggest changes in tense and word choice, and perhaps rewrite entire sentences. Most will not rewrite paragraphs, however, unless given
permission to do so in advance.

Qualified copy editors vary wildly in price. Some will charge you
many thousands of dollars depending on the complexity of your project,
the strength of their own pedigree, or the size of your wallet. Evaluate
them carefully by sending portions of your book to several editors.
Most will be willing to edit a page or two of your book and send you a
"markup version" of these pages. This version will show you every single
change they have made. If you really want to get an "apples-to-apples"
comparison between potential editors, ask them to edit the same page or

two and then compare their markups. You will probably see significant differences between the editors in regard to style and attention to detail. Use this information to make your selection.

Interior Design/Layout

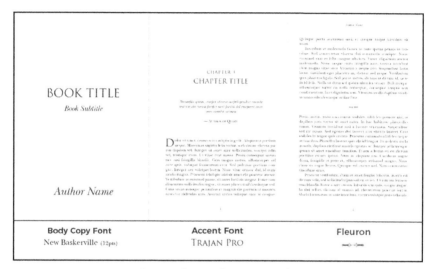

Interior layout design example

Another area of critical import is the interior layout of your book. The proper interior layout is the difference between a polished and professional book vs. a glorified Word document. Unfortunately, I have seen far too many self-published books that look like a freshman term paper. (I used to teach freshman English at a university, so I know!)

You have taken the time to write a quality book. Don't blow it with a cruddy layout. We always employ a professional layout artist to make sure that margins, headers, footers, footnotes, etc. are perfect. Honestly, there are an incredible number of important details when it comes to layout. While margins and headers are obvious ones, little details make a difference. Seemingly small details like the size and position of page numbers can change the appearance of a page. Done properly, interior layout should result in a completed manuscript that looks like a professionally produced book, because it is precisely that: a professionally produced book. But poor layout can make all your hard work look amateurish. And an amatuer look can destroy all the credibility you are working so hard to establish.

As in other areas of publishing, layout services can vary dramatically in price. Look for an expert who has an excellent track record. Consider also whether they can work according to your timeline and whether they will be there to respond to change requests. Many designers will allow a limited number of revisions or drafts. You should plan to pay a bit extra for time you go beyond the agreed-upon number of drafts. Beware of a designer who promises "unlimited revisions" as well as ones who work for a very small fee. Logic dictates that no provider can provide truly unlimited revisions. There is always a point at which a designer will no longer work for the original fee. More often than not, the designer who promises unlimited revisions falls off the face of the earth at some point. Communication slows and then stops. This is also true for the designer who works for a song. For this reason, choose your designer carefully, consider his or her track record, and look at examples of his or her work. We also recommend you seek the final files when layout is done. These are usually in the form of InDesign files, documents developed using Adobe's InDesign software.

Artwork

If there is one area in which you absolutely should not skimp, it is your cover artwork! If you were to tell me that you could afford to pay for either editing, layout, or cover artwork, I would pick the cover artwork every time.

Why? It's very simple. Look back to all my discussion about the impact of a book that is never read. Remember that? I went on and on about how a book absolutely oozes authority and how the presence of your name on the book by itself makes you the go-to expert in the eyes of your prospects and clients. And I talked about the durability of a book and its impact even just sitting on a shelf. Well, if you put a poorly designed cover on your book, you can throw all that away! In fact, a cruddy cover will have the opposite effect. Rather than help establish your authority, it will diminish it. So don't skimp here.

Plan to hire a professional artist to design your cover, but make sure your artist is experienced with book covers. You may know a great artist who you have hired to make your logo or design your website, but don't count on that artist to make a professional-looking book cover. You also need to make sure your artist conforms to proper artwork specifications in regard to color formulation (CMYK and not RGB), resolution (300 dpi or better), bleed (usually ⅛"), margins, safe zones, UPC/ISBN code placement, etc. If you don't understand some or all of these terms, that's fine. You don't have to. But your artist better!

No matter how great any artist is, this artist can give you input from only one brain: his or her own. For this reason, I recommend you get cover concepts from multiple artists. Even though we have access to dozens of great cover artists, we never rely on the work of only one. In fact, we never use only two or three. Instead, we employ a process that allows us to seek design concepts from a dozen or more artists. By the time we are done with our cover design process, we usually have 50+ design concepts. This range of choices allows us to create the best possible cover.

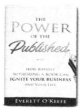

5 out of 108 variations for *The Power of the Published*

In fact, we employed the same cover creation process for *The Power of the Published*. It resulted in 108 cover concepts by 16 artists from all around the world. Working through all these variations can be a lot of work, but it is also a lot of fun. More significantly, your cover is arguably the most important part of your book. A great cover goes a long way for covering failings in other areas, but the reverse is not true. Don't cut corners here!

Publishing

The process of publishing your book is beyond the scope of this book. There are simply too many details and considerations involved in the publishing process to handle here. If you are a die-hard do-it-yourselfer who wants to publish your book on a shoestring budget, then there are other books available to help you along your way.

On the other hand, if giving your book the DIY treatment is not appealing, then you most certainly understand the value of hiring someone who has the expertise to carry out the entire process in an effective manner. You likely know where your gifts are best utilized, and perhaps editing, layout, artwork, and publishing are not your gifts. If that is the case, consider using what is called a hybrid publishing company to bring your book to market.

In the final chapters, I will explain the many benefits of self-publishing, especially as they compare to the traditional publishing process. I will also discuss the benefits of hybrid publishing, which essentially allows you to enjoy all the positives of self-publishing without having to do all the work yourself.

19

SELF-PUBLISHING

We are in the golden age of self-publishing. With the advent of Amazon and other online bookstores, we are experiencing the true democratization of publishing. The launch of the Kindle book format in 2007 is credited with making publishing accessible and affordable for the first time. Only a dozen years ago, most publishing was limited to a handful of big publishing houses and a larger group of expensive "vanity press" companies. These companies collectively held the purse strings of the industry, largely determining who would be published and what messages would be brought to the marketplace.

But even before the launch of Kindle and the various online portals we have today, self-publishing had a unique role. Books that were rejected by publishers could be self-published in defiance of the status quo. Though the process of self-publishing was often wildly expensive and difficult, authors sometimes bucked the conventions of the industry and had success despite their rejections.

Beatrix Potter self-published *The Tale of Peter Rabbit* in 1901 after repeated rejections by traditional publishing companies. She ultimately paid to have 250 copies of her book printed and set about promoting it. Her book was incredibly successful, to the point that it was picked up by one of the publishers that had turned her down previously. By the end of the next year, over 20,000 copies had been sold.

By the way, she self-published her next book too, after her publisher refused to print the book according to her specifications. This time, she printed 500 copies and sold them on her own. Her publisher later caved in and printed her books the way she demanded.[9]

Many other famous authors have employed self-publishing. Virginia Woolf, e. e. Cummings, Edgar Allan Poe, and Mark Twain all used self-publishing. Even Stephen King self-published a collection of short stories prior to releasing *Carrie*, his first traditionally published book.[10]

Margaret Atwood (author of *The Handmaid's Tale*) self-published her first book of poetry *Double Persephone*. She printed 220 copies by herself, and it was an immediate success. Her book later won the E.J. Pratt Medal and paved the way for her other works.[11]

Fortunately, self-publishing is much easier now. Technology has facilitated self-publishing at an unprecedented level. Here are some more recent success stories.

Perhaps you have seen the movie *The Martian*, starring Matt Damon. You may not know that the book upon which it is based, *The Martian* by Andy Weir, was originally self-published. Word has it that Weir did his research and determined he would never get a traditional publisher to take on his book. So, he posted the book, a chapter at a time, on his blog. It started to gain followers. He later published the completed version as a 99-cent Kindle on Amazon. The book became extremely popular, to the point that a publisher took on the book and paid Weir $100,000 for the privilege.[12] I have no idea what the movie rights cost!

Fifty Shades of Grey started off self-published. E. L. James started publishing these racy books by herself in 2011. *Fifty Shades* has since become a huge brand with book sales and movie deals far in excess of all but the most successful traditionally published books.[13]

The Shack by William P. Young was rejected by publishers 26 times before the author decided to take matters into his own hands. It ultimately became a New York Times #1 bestseller and a major motion picture.[14]

You may or may not have heard of Meredith Wild. She is known in some circles as the author of the erotic Hacker novels. She is known in other circles as the author who acquired a $7 million publishing deal after self-publishing her first four books. She has sold over 1.2 million eBooks and in excess of 200,000 print-on-demand paperbacks![15]

There are countless self-publishing success stories. I have only highlighted a few. I bring these to your attention so you will understand that self-publishing is a highly successful and reputable way to bring a book to market. In the past, self-publishing was considered the realm of the rejected by the publishing industry, unworthy of acceptance by the self-proclaimed experts of the industry. Now, these same publishing experts are combing the rolls of self-published books, looking for the next *Fifty Shades of Grey* or *The Martian*.

Why is this happening? What advantages does self-publishing hold? There are several benefits:

Green Light

Did you know that the first Harry Potter book was initially rejected by multiple publishing agents and approximately a dozen publishers? J. K. Rowling continued to push her book, and it was finally accepted by Bloomsbury (who paid her only £1,500, by the way!).[16] Somewhere along the line, someone told her "not to quit her day job."[17]

In fact, rejection is a common theme for many successful writers. Let's take a look:

- Stephen King's *Carrie*, rejected 30 times
- *The Lord of the Flies* by William Golding, rejected 20 times
- John le Carré's *The Spy Who Came in from the Cold*, rejected with the admonition that he "hasn't got any future"
- *Gone with the Wind* by Margaret Mitchell, rejected 38 times
- *The Diary of a Young Girl* by Anne Frank, rejected 15 times

- Louisa May Alcott (*Little Women*) was told teaching would be better
- *Dune* by Frank Herbert, 23 rejections
- *Dubliners* by James Joyce, 22 rejections
- *Zen and the Art of Motorcycle Maintenance* by Robert Pirsig, tops this list with 121 rejections![18]

I could go on and on with this list, but I think you get the point. Most (maybe all!) famous authors have met with rejection.

I was once told by a publishing executive that the large publishing houses take on only 80 projects a year. That represents a very small fraction of the book proposals they receive every year. As a result, very few authors receive a green light for their books. Such publishers use their own criteria for accepting and rejecting projects. First and foremost, they have to determine if they (not the author) will make money. To make money, the author must have a very large and passionate following, also known as the author's "platform." This is a combination of followers on social media, blog subscribers, purchasers of previous books, and people for whom the author has email addresses. If the author has a large enough platform, they will have no problem finding a publisher. But if they lack fame and following, the odds of getting a traditional publishing deal are very small.

Traditional publishers remind me a bit of that saying about banks: they will only loan you money when you don't need it. Publishers are more than happy to take you on when you no longer need them! And who can blame them? Like a bank, they must do their best to make a profit, and when they back such a small number of books a year, they have to be very discriminating.

As such, it is extremely hard to get the green light for a traditional publishing deal.

Obviously, this is not the case with self-publishing. Self-publishing requires no permission. You do not have to shop a book idea to countless disinterested publishers and get their seal of approval. *You* determine if your project is worth it. *You* decide if your message is valuable. *You* decide if your project gets the green light!

Speed to Market

It can take years to bring a book to market through traditional publishing companies. Provided your book is picked up by one of these companies, the typical turnaround time is 18 months or more. This allows time for development, revisions, drafts, edits, publishing. *Wow, 18 months!* This assumes, of course, that your book has already been accepted. Many authors spend years shopping

> Do you have years to wait before putting the power of a book to work for you?

their book before it gets accepted. Many more spend years and *never* get accepted.

Do you have years to wait before putting the power of a book to work for you?

On the other hand, there are few speed bumps on the road to self-publishing. What traditional publishing companies accomplish in 18 months can be completed in under *three or four* months via self-publishing. Large, corporate wheels turn slowly, and many decisions are made by committee with meeting after meeting. In self-publishing, decisions are made instantly and put into play almost as quickly. As a result, authors who utilize self-publishing often see their books launched to the world while their traditionally published counterparts are still reviewing cover options!

Print-on-Demand

I love technology. And one of the most wonderful technological achieve-ments to hit the publishing world is "print-on-demand." Heck, I think it is right up there with compound interest! Like the name implies, books configured in this way are printed only as demand dictates. More specifically, books are printed only after they are sold! In fact, Amazon's print-on-demand service is incredible. A customer buys your book from Amazon today. Within 24 hours, Amazon prints that single copy of your book and ships it to your customer. Amazon deducts the printing cost and pays you a royalty based on the difference! Could it be easier?

In the past, you could always know a self-published author by vis-iting his or her garage. Ten years after they published their book, you would still find cases of books sitting there! This is simply because they had to buy cases upon cases of books just to get a reasonable per-copy printing price.

No longer!

With print-on-demand, you have no need to invest thousands of dollars in inventory. Instead, you can simply order the number of "au-thor copies" you need whenever you need them. There is no minimum print run, and the per-copy price is very affordable, often under $3 a book. This means you can order one or 500 books, and you can have them drop-shipped wherever you like. This is especially good if you are traveling to a speaking engagement or trade show. Your books can meet you there!

Author copies are also available through traditional publishing. Most publishing agreements include a provision wherein the author can get books at a discount that varies from roughly 50% to 75% depending on quantity. One contract I reviewed included this language:

Author's discount off the suggested retail price shall be: 55% for 1–100 copies; 60% for 101–500 copies; 65% for 501–1,000 cop-ies; and 75% for all copies over 1,000.

Based on a cover price of $15, according to this contract, you would have to order one thousand copies to get the author price down to $3.75, and this is *still* more expensive than print-on-demand! In addition, this is limited to stock on-hand. If the publisher is out of inventory, they will not print more except as part of a (much larger) print run associated with the next printing, something that only occurs if you are selling lots of books. This is simply not a problem with print-on-demand, where the needed stock can always be printed on the fly.

Not only do traditional publishers charge you more for author copies, they also limit the ways you may use them! While some contracts will allow you to sell such books at a table associated with a book signing, you generally cannot place them for sale in any bookstore or retailer. Understandably, the publisher does not want you to be in competition with them. Their core business is selling books to retailers, and they don't want you doing the same. Most authors won't run afoul of this, but this can be a problem if you want to sell books through an event bookstore or at an organization's office.

Frank Leyes has published three books through Ignite Press, and each has been configured for print-on-demand. When he was asked by Dan Sullivan's Strategic Coach organization to provide books for sale in its company bookstore, this was no problem at all because of the self-published nature of his books. We simply had author copies printed and shipped directly to the store. Had Frank gone the traditional publishing route, this might not have been an option. Even if it were possible, the author copies would have cost roughly twice as much, which would have cut into the profits of both Frank and the store.

Simply put, print-on-demand technology is a game changer for any author. It allows you to order and receive copies of your own book with a speed and price point that was previously unknown. It is an incredible advantage for the self-published author.

Creative Control

We tend to think of arguments about creative control in terms of Hollywood directors and actors, arguing about how a character should be portrayed. If you are like me, you might think fairly negatively about such arguments. But creative control as it applies to your book is something entirely different.

In a traditional publishing environment, you sacrifice a certain amount of control over your product. This is simply because you no longer *own* your project! You sold those rights, remember? Here is a quote from the publishing contract of a large publisher:

> *All details of publications of Physical Versions and Digital Versions, including manufacturing, format and design, distribution, pricing, advertising and promotion and dissemination of free copies, will be determined by Publisher.*

The first two words say it all: "all details." While the publisher may agree to consult with the author on any number of issues, they are under no obligation to abide by the author's wishes unless spelled out in the agreement.

The publisher owns the rights, and they have one goal: make money. If they think a change to your book would help them make more money, they can (and will) do it. This may be fine if the main goal is to sell copies of your book to make royalties. As you know from reading this book, however, royalties are about the least profitable way to use a book! In your profession, you are likely to make far more by leveraging your book and the authority it gives you.

This is why creative control is critical. You know your business far better than any publisher. There is no committee at a publishing house that understands your clients and prospects better than you do! What's more, you understand better than they how you can use your book and its message to change lives. Self-publishing, whether accomplished through a DIY approach or with a hybrid publisher, allows you to maintain complete creative control.

Intellectual Property

Self-publishing allows you to maintain all the rights to your intellectual property. This is essential. Your book may be the single-largest document you ever create, and it is likely filled with your stories, ideas, and strategies. For you to successfully leverage your own content, you need to *own* that content, and you need to be able to freely exercise that control.

Traditional publishers typically pay authors an advance (small or large) when a publishing agreement is reached. This is paid to compensate the author for selling his or her intellectual property rights to the publisher. Sadly, many authors sell far more of their rights than they realize in the process. Many writers have discovered after the fact that they sold movie rights and other important rights with the original contract. For this reason, should you ever find yourself working with a traditional publisher, make sure to have an intellectual property rights attorney *that you hire* review any contracts!

Even when your agreement allows you to maintain limited rights to your content, you may find you can only exercise those rights in certain outlets. For instance, you may have the right to use the content in speeches and radio appearances but find yourself handcuffed when you want to use it in another book, article, or video. If you want to make an audiobook of your content or create a PBS special, you will likely have to negotiate with your publisher (and include them in the deal).

In self-publishing, none of this is an issue. You maintain all the rights to your ideas and content, and you maintain the ability to use those ideas and content in any way you wish. Want to create an audio version of your book? Great. Want to share a chapter or two as a download from your website? No problem. Do what you want, when you want, in whatever way you want.

If you take advantage of the many benefits of a *hybrid* publisher, make sure your rights are fully protected. Here is a section from our publishing contract:

> *Agency warrants to the fullest extent possible under law, that Client shall own any and all right, title and interest, including copyrights, and other intellectual property rights, with respect to any copy, photograph, advertisement, content (articles, videos, press releases, blog posts, etc...), or other work or material created by Agency or at Agency's direction for Client under this agreement.*

You will notice that the author (referred to here as "Client") keeps all the rights to the book and any artwork, images, and even promotional material created to market the book. You should expect the same from any hybrid publisher you might employ.

Royalties

Royalties are simply a share of the proceeds from book sales. In traditional and self-publishing, authors are usually paid a percentage of the sale prices for any book that is sold. While many budding authors have dreams of nice, fat royalty checks arriving in their mailboxes, this is usually not the case. In fact, most authors make little to no money from royalties.

Royalties from traditional publishing companies vary, but I have seen them as low as 8.5% and as high as 24%. The percentage on e-books (Kindle, Kobo, etc) is often around 25%. Many times, the actual royalty will start lower for the initial 10,000 to 20,000 of physical book sales and then bump up afterward. Given that most books never sell more than the initial threshold amount, authors are often paid royalties at the lower portion of the royalty range and never get to the higher percentages.

Keep in mind that royalties are only paid after any advance has been earned. In other words, if an author is given a $10,000 advance to sign the publishing agreement, the initial royalties that would otherwise go to the author are kept by the company until they exceed the advance. For example, let's assume an author's book is priced at $15, and he or she is to get a 15% royalty. That equals $2.25 per book. If the author was paid a $10,000 advance, 4,444 books must be sold before any additional money is to be paid to the author. That is a lot of books. Book *returns* must be factored in too, making it even harder for the author to earn substantial money from royalties.

Royalties are higher and more accessible in self-publishing. Whereas traditional publishers may pay 8.5% to 24% royalties, depending on the number of books sold, many self-published authors earn a 60% royalty from the very first copy. This 60% is paid after deducting printing costs. A 150-page paperback book on Amazon's platform would cost $2.65 to print. If the selling price is $15, a 60% royalty equals $7.41 a copy! Compare that to $2.25 royalty with traditional publishing.

The difference is even more dramatic with e-books/Kindle. Whereas traditional publishers will pay as much as a 25% royalty for e-books, Amazon's Kindle Direct Publishing platform will pay you up to 70%! It firsts deduct a (minimal) digital delivery charge. For example, a Kindle book priced at $9.99 would pay a royalty of $6.96 after a 4-cent delivery charge! These numbers are all subject to change, of course, but I think you get the point. The royalty percentages available in self-publishing far exceed those paid by traditional publishers.

For this reason, even hugely successful, traditionally-published authors sometimes leverage self-publishing. Rachel Hollis is the New York Times #1 bestselling author of *Girl, Wash Your Face* and *Girl, Stop Apologizing*. Both books are currently in the top five of all books on Amazon and have been for some time. Although she has been wildly successful as a traditionally-published author, she self-publishes a series of journals to support her brand. At a recent conference, she announced that she makes more money from the self-published journals (which are super easy to develop, by the way!) than she does from her blockbuster books! This is largely because she gets to keep all the royalties rather than sharing profit with a publisher!

This being said, I consider royalties to simply be "icing on the cake" for most of my authors. Unless you already have a huge following, you are unlikely to make any substantial money in book sales. In any case, the power of the published is far greater than any small check that might be paid by Amazon or some other service. As we have seen in earlier chapters, royalties pale in comparison to the many other benefits of publishing. As I like to tell people, you won't make money *on* your book, but you are likely to make a ton *through* your book!

Bestseller Launch

Most traditional publishers do not understand an Amazon bestseller launch. Or if they understand it, they rarely pursue it. Part of the reason is that they cannot afford to favor one retailer over another. Although Amazon is the largest bookseller in the world, if the publisher favors Amazon over other outlets, the other outlets may stop carrying their books. In addition, our favored strategy for launching books centers around the Kindle version of the book because of pricing and category flexibility that simply does not exist with printed versions. Traditional publishers fail to satisfactorily promote Kindle and other e-book formats because they interfere with their goal of selling printed books. When a publisher prepares for a book launch, they print a predetermined number of books. Their greatest fear is to get stuck with large numbers of these books.

> You won't make money *on* your book, but you are likely to make a ton *through* your book!

As a result, they don't want to do anything that may take away from print sales.

The self-published author has no such qualms or limitations! Because books are printed through print-on-demand technology, books are only printed after they are sold. Therefore, there is no inventory to store, and there is no investment in a large print run. This freedom allows you, the author (along with any hybrid publisher), to focus on the Kindle launch!

We have had numerous authors come to us after publishing their book through traditional means. Each one has been underwhelmed by their experience with traditional publishing. They all expected their publisher would do more to promote their books, and they thought a traditional publisher was an avenue to media exposure, a book tour, and a chance to be a bestselling author. At the end of the day, they shared their frustrations about an overall lack of support and unmet expectations.

Many decided to leverage self-publishing for their next books. What's more, they asked us to create coordinated bestseller launches so they could experience both the freedom of self-publishing and the authority that comes with bestseller status, something their traditional publisher could not (or would not) provide.

Bestseller launches, by the way, are not reserved for those authors with huge numbers of followers or large email lists. I have seen highly successful launches from authors who started with essentially no list. When we started working with Molly Claire on *The Happy Mom Mindset*, she had only a very small email list of clients, friends, and family. We set her up with some list-building tools and strategies, and she went to work on those while we worked on publishing her book. By the time the launch date came around, Molly had developed a more extensive and very passionate list of followers eager to buy her book. As a result, she became a #1 bestselling author.

In the end, a bestseller launch is more about passion than numbers anyway. Huge lists are often dispassionate, which may be why traditional publishers struggle here and why self-published authors shine. One only has to look at the fans of *50 Shades of Grey* or *The Martian* to see the results of this passion.

The Final Word on Self-Publishing

I have spelled out seven distinct and important advantages to self-publishing. Altogether, they make compelling case for handling all of your publishing details on your own. But who has the time or expertise to do everything that must be done? Fortunately, there is a solution, as you will see in the next chapter.

20

HYBRID PUBLISHING

The Best of Both Worlds

While self-publishing has numerous advantages, there is one serious disadvantage. You can see it in the very term: *self*-publishing. Self-publishing in the purest sense relies upon you to carry out the entire publishing process. In addition to creating the manuscript, it's also up to you to get it edited, find and supervise a professional interior layout artist, create or source a professional cover, and complete the myriad steps to make your book available for printing, distribution, and marketing. These steps include (among others) keyword research, category research, pricing, creation of the book description, ISBN registration (where appropriate), proofing, graphic configuration, and much, much more. The details are many, and getting even one of them wrong can cause frustration and complication.

And all this occurs before you can even consider a bestseller launch, which, as we discussed above, even many traditional publishing companies appear unable or unwilling to perform properly.

For this reason, there is a third type of publishing: hybrid publishing. Hybrid publishing allows you to enjoy all of the advantages of self-publishing without having to do all the work! By engaging with what is called a "hybrid publisher," you get to remove the "self" from the majority of the post-writing work. Rather than having to find a way to complete all phases of manuscript preparation, artwork development, publishing, distribution, and launch, you engage with a company that is experienced in all aspects of the process, and team completes these tasks for you.

These companies are called hybrid because they handle all the details and work of publishing your book like a traditional publisher, but you typically retain some or all the rights to your content and receive higher royalties like in self-publishing.

A hybrid publishing company should be able to handle all or nearly all aspects of bringing your book to market. Some will work with you to develop your initial book concept and guide you along the road to writing your manuscript. Others will only work with you when your manuscript is complete. Some will provide a soup-to-nuts approach, providing all the services needed to publish your book. Such companies may provide copy or line editing, interior layout, cover design, publishing, and even book launch services. Others are more limited in their offerings, focusing solely on placing your book for sale at various online outlets.

> Hybrid publishing allows you to enjoy all of the advantages of self-publishing without having to do all the work!

Unlike traditional publishers, many hybrid publishers do not make money from book sales. All royalties flow directly to you. There is no middleman between you and your sales. As a result, many hybrid publishers operate on a fee-for-service basis.

Some hybrid publishers, however, operate a bit more like traditional publishers. Although they take a fee upfront, they *also* take a portion of sales. They may also apply a markup for author copies. The same paperback that might cost you $3 otherwise may be made available to you for $5 instead. While I have no objection to this model if properly disclosed, this type of hybrid publisher takes away some of the best advantages to self-publishing—in this case, higher royalties and lower cost of author copies.

A word of caution. If you hire a hybrid publishing company, determine in advance two more things: First, will you own all of the rights to your content? Second, will you have an easy and affordable way to exercise those rights? Let me explain.

Some hybrid publishing companies take the approach of traditional publishers where they have you sign over all or part of the rights to your book and/or brand. They may demand exclusive rights to distribution, force you to buy author copies through them (at a marked-up cost), or otherwise limit (or eliminate) your ability to take your content and publish it elsewhere. This may be completely understandable in the case of a traditional publisher who has perhaps paid you a sizeable advance in exchange for these rights. In my opinion, this is *not* acceptable in the case of a hybrid publisher that you have paid to publish your book! If a company pays you to buy the rights to your intellectual property, that's fine. But you should never have to sacrifice your intellectual property rights without proper compensation.

Even if a company makes it clear that you own all the rights to your content, it may make it expensive or difficult to exercise these rights. For instance, the company may charge a substantial fee to provide you with the source files for your book. It may charge a hefty change fee if you want to make even a small change to your online book description or alter the price of your Kindle. While it is completely understandable for a company to charge a reasonable fee because of labor costs it incurs to make changes to a book, some companies seem to put charges in place to actively discourage authors from utilizing the rights to their own content.

For this reason, we adopt a completely different approach at Ignite Press. After we have published and launched your book, we provide our clients with all the files associated with their book. We send them the interior layout files along with the Kindle/e-book files. We send them the layered cover artwork so it can be easily edited if needed. We even send a list of logins for all accounts where the book is hosted. If we perform a bestseller launch, we also send a thorough launch report and screenshots to document the results.

A business coach of mine once told me that we should handle things entirely in the opposite fashion. He told me that we should be like a utility company for our clients. Just like we all have to go through the utility company to get our electricity, he said our publishing clients should have to go through us for everything related to their books, at an expense, of course. Well, that is not how we choose to work.

This is how I work.

If you work with us to publish your book and you want to do something else with your content later on, no problem. We provide all your files and logins to facilitate the free exercise of your rights. On the other hand, if you want us to help you on other projects in the future, we stand ready. Ultimately, we only want to work with people who *want* to work with us.

I recommend you look for that kind of treatment wherever you go and whatever you do. No one deserves to have their book held hostage, and everyone deserves the right to take their business where they want. It just makes sense.

Whatever You Do…

Whatever you do and *however* you choose to do it, write your book. Get it out to the world. The world deserves to hear your message and to learn from your wisdom. Your accumulated knowledge needs to be shared. Whether you decide to publish by yourself or with a hybrid publisher or if you choose to wade in the challenging waters of traditional publishing, the power of the published awaits you.

CONCLUSION

Take a couple of deep breaths, and dream with me for a minute:

It's late on a Thursday afternoon. You have been waiting expectantly all day. You are tempted to log in to the FedEx site yet again to check the tracking status on your package, but you resist. All day, you have been hoping to see the FedEx truck pull up in front of your office. Heck, you feel like a kid waiting for Santa to arrive.

Five o'clock comes and goes. Then five-thirty. Finally, knowing you have to leave, you start to lock up the office.

Just then, you hear it. You hear the rumble of a truck pulling into the complex. You look up as a parcel truck pulls in front of your office. Not content to wait at your office door, you step to the curb to meet the truck. The driver greets you at the open door of the truck, asks your name, and says, "I think I have something for you!"

He hands you a medium-sized box. It's heavy. Solid.

Expectantly, you carry the box into your office. You don't even bother carrying it back to the conference room. Instead, you drop it right there on the receptionist's desk and reach for the scissors. Carefully, you cut open the box and pull back the flaps. At first, all you see is the brown paper lining the box and covering its contents. But beneath a flap in the paper, you see what you have been waiting for. You catch a glimpse of a book. *Your* book!

You peel back the paper to see two glossy stacks of your book. You pause.

This isn't the first time you have seen this cover. You've looked at it over and over on your computer, reviewing drafts from the artist and your publisher. You have even seen 3D renders of your cover.

But this is different. This is *for real.*

You pick up a copy of the book. *Your book.* It feels solid in your hand. There is weight to it.

Looking at the cover, you look at the colors, the print. You pause as you look at your name in large, broad letters. *Your* name on the cover of a book!

Your hands tingle slightly as you turn the book over. Your eye is immediately drawn to your picture, your headshot. Your bio, with all your greatest accomplishments, sits next to it. Yes, this is your book, and you never thought you would see this day.

Sure, you have thought for years that you might write a book someday. Someday. But years and more years went by without any serious step toward completing a book. It was always going to happen "someday." Well, "someday" has arrived.

You turn the book and look at the spine. Seeing your book title above your name is almost surreal. With your thumbs, you open the book and fan through the pages. The typeface is clear. The text goes on and on.

Now, *this* is real. These are your words. Your ideas, page after page of them.

It finally sinks in. This really is your book. A feeling of pride begins to well up in you, a sense of accomplishment. At long last, you've done it.

And it feels *so* good.

If you have never experienced the joy of holding your own book for the very first time, take it from me: It is an amazing experience. My first instinct is to compare it to sitting in the seat of your very first car for the first time. But I think it is better than that. Sitting in your first car may have brought you a sense of joy, but it's not the same thing as holding your book for the first time. What if you worked and saved for every dollar to buy that car? Now you are getting closer. The feeling of accomplishment at *earning* the car combined with the joy of *having* the car is a wonderful experience. But it takes one more step.

I think the experience is akin to the day I earned my pilot's license. I had worked on that license for more than a year. I completed lengthy ground school classes, studied textbooks, labored over maps and calculations, memorized weather patterns, and much more. I spent hours in the air, grinding out stalls, steep turns, and emergency landing approaches in the hot Central California skies. I worked hard to gain my pilot's license.

But it wasn't just the hard work that made my accomplishment special. It was the hard work combined with the fact that I had joined an elite fraternity, a small group of people who had struggled like I had and gained the right to fly an aircraft through the sky! I had earned the right to jump in an airplane, fire up the motor, and fly anywhere those wings would take me. I could sail through the clouds and look down on the earth far below, knowing I had accomplished something that very few others would accomplish.

Can you imagine how that feels? Can you begin to understand the experience? If so, then you are beginning to understand what it feels like to hold your book in your hand for the first time. It is the joy of *having* your own book, combined with the fact that you have *earned* the accomplishment and have now joined the *elite* community of authors. These three factors make authorship a powerful experience.

However, as you have read, authorship is more than a powerful experience. The power of the published goes far beyond a feeling of accomplishment at having attained a status that few ever will. It is also about putting the power of a book to work in your business or organization; it is about employing the most powerful single tool available to increase visibility, create authority, convert prospects, and retain clients. The power of the published is potent. And it is a power that I hope you experience in the very near future.

Will You Experience the Power of the Published?

If you have read this far, you understand the incredible power of a book. When will you get to experience it firsthand? The odds are extremely high that you have considered writing a book for quite some time, to ignite a spark in your business or to share some intensely important message.

Stop dreaming about it.

I have worked with dozens of authors who dreamed for years about a writing book and failed, year after year, to make it happen. Then, with my guidance, these same authors quickly saw their dreams come to life in the form of a book. A bestselling book.

What would it mean for you to have a bestselling book next quarter? What would it mean for your business?

It's possible. It really can be done. And it doesn't require you to sequester yourself and neglect your work or your family. It just requires some help.

I have shown you how it can be done.

I have shown you *why* it should be done.

Now let us help you *do* it.

Every year, Ignite Press takes on a limited number of publishing clients. If you would like to discuss a book with us, you can schedule a complimentary book consultation through our website at https://

IgnitePress.us. There is no obligation, and this might just start you on the path to authorship.

See you soon!

Everett O'Keefe
Clovis, California

ENDNOTES

1. https://en.wikipedia.org/wiki/The_Beatles_in_Hamburg

2. https://www.statista.com/topics/1244/physicians

3. https://www.creditdonkey.com/buyers-remorse.html

4. https://www.psychologytoday.com/us/blog/wishful-thoughts/201708/buyer-s-remorse

5. https://www.forbes.com/sites/kathycaprino/2016/10/11/the-worlds-leading-high-performance-coach-shares-3-steps-for-breaking-bad-habits/#5e34992c3ad4

6. https://www.bigspeak.com/speakers/brendon-burchard/

7. https://en.wikipedia.org/wiki/Rachel_Hollis

8. https://examples.yourdictionary.com/examples-of-catalysts.html

9. https://www.theguardian.com/books/booksblog/2013/dec/17/beatrix-potter-peter-rabbit-self-publishing

10. https://indiereader.com/2016/10/6-famous-authors-chose-self-publish/

11. https://electricliterature.com/11-books-that-prove-theres-nothing-wrong-with-self-publishing/

12. https://writingcooperative.com/3-self-published-authors-who-went-on-to-have-mainstream-success-and-how-they-did-it-36ce6dc4512f

13. https://www.dorrancepublishing.com/notable-self-published-authors/

14. https://electricliterature.com/11-books-that-prove-theres-nothing-wrong-with-self-publishing/

15. https://writingcooperative.com/3-self-published-authors-who-went-on-to-have-mainstream-success-and-how-they-did-it-36ce6dc4512f

16. http://barbararogan.com/blog/?p=29

17. https://www.buzzfeed.com/stmartinspress/20-brilliant-authors-whose-work-was-initially-reje-7rut

18. https://www.buzzfeed.com/stmartinspress/20-brilliant-authors-whose-work-was-initially-reje-7rut

ABOUT THE AUTHOR

Everett O'Keefe is a Wall Street Journal, USA Today, and International #1 Bestselling Author. As the founder of Ignite Press—a hybrid publishing company specializing in helping entrepreneurs, business people, and medical professionals ignite their businesses by becoming bestselling authors—Everett and his team have helped create and launch more than 95 bestselling books for his clients. In addition, Everett loves to speak across the nation on the power of publishing.

Everett is the winner of multiple awards, including the Publish and Profit Award for Excellence in Publishing, the Make Market & Launch It Award for Product Creation, and the Top Gun Consulting Award, among others. He is the co-founder of the Business Accelerator Group, a high-level mastermind group composed of international marketers and publishers. He also helped found the Mastermind Retreat and continues to host international mastermind events.

Sought out as a speaker, coach, and consultant by authors and marketing experts worldwide, Everett has a passion for entrepreneurialism. By helping his clients become recognized experts in their fields through speaking and authorship—with their bestselling books in hand—he supports them in sharing their gifts with a growing audience.

You can reach Everett through his company's website at
https://IgnitePress.us.
Everett can also be found on social media at these sites:
https://www.facebook.com/ignitepress/
https://www.linkedin.com/in/everettokeefe/
For the Business Accelerator Group and Everett's mastermind retreats,
visit http://MastermindRetreat.net.

May I Ask a Favor?

You can determine a great deal of a book's success by adding to the number and nature of the reviews online. These reviews guide other readers to discover books that help them along their journeys.

    If you have found value in this book, please consider leaving an honest review at an online bookstore. If you purchased the book, please place your comments at that site. If this book was a gift, you could add your review at any major online retailer.

    I greatly appreciate your honest feedback and reviews.

Everett O'Keefe
Clovis, California

WHAT PEOPLE ARE SAYING ABOUT IGNITE PRESS

As a Green Beret combat veteran about to leave two decades of military service, I felt as if I were changing planets. Anxiety was an understatement! I learned a lot of painful lessons on my military transition journey—lessons that needed to be shared with other veterans.

I knew I had a story to tell. And that my story could change lives.

But I was stuck. While I knew my story and my message, I had no clue how to get that story out into the world. If that story stayed inside of me, the veterans who needed to hear my story would be cheated out of it.

Everett fully understood the sacred nature of this work and took on the project of editing, formatting, publishing, and launching my book *Mission America* with the care and loyalty of a patriot and friend.

I write this today as the author of a #1 international bestseller.

I don't recommend many folks these days simply because authenticity and tradecraft are hard to come by. Recommending Everett O'Keefe for any of your life's work, however, is the easiest thing I could ever do.

He is—and will always be—my trusted source and teammate for content that changes lives.

Scott Mann
Green Beret, International #1 Bestselling Author
Warrior Storyteller
President of Rooftop Leadership

* * *

I created *The Retirement GPS* with Everett and the Ignite Press team to enhance my professional standing. I have been teaching a retirement planning class for 14 years and have been practicing financial planning for 36. All this time, I have been looking for a way to increase my credibility with new prospects. At the same time, I wanted to encapsulate my planning concepts and provide an additional resource for those who are seeking a guide along the financial highway to retirement. I had never written a book before, so I needed lots of help and guidance to complete this monumental project. I could not have done it without the help of Everett and the entire team at Ignite Press.

Now that my book is complete and we have made it a bestseller, I couldn't be more pleased. The feedback from clients who have read the book has been stupendous. Thanks to the way Everett had me craft the book, they tell me they enjoyed reading it, found great value in the contents, and also found that it was not too technical or over their heads. We now use our book as a resource and credibility tool for new clients and new class participants. We also use it in our community to gain access to larger employers and more valuable clients. I give the team at Ignite Press a 100,000-kilowatt award for all of their support.

Chuck Bigbie, CLU ChFC CFP
#1 Bestselling Author
Woodland Wealth Management, Inc.

* * *

Although I have written two books previously, the books that have given me the most joy to produce were the last three. For each of these books, Everett and his team gave me a format, a timeline, a direction, a hug, and (when needed) a few good-natured shoves. They laid down a track on which I could run.

I have now done three books with Everett's assistance, and each one has become a bestseller. This accomplishment is significant because being an international #1 bestselling author has provided me with a platform to share my message. It is different from others who wave their manuscripts yelling, "I wrote a book," and wanting a parade. I'm a #1 bestselling author with a screenshot that shows I've knocked *Good to Great* out of first place! No one can ever take that from me.

Being an author opens conversations. Being a published author opens doors. Being a *bestselling* author gives credibility that few people in the world have and so many ache for.

I'm good at what I do. And I'm smart enough to know that a great coach will help me get better. Working with Everett was like being re-assured that if we stayed on the path, no wild animals would get us. Having someone like Everett in my corner, functioning as my coach, my guide on this crazy and wonderful journey, is worth it in so many ways.

When it comes time to write my next book (and it is coming soon!), there will be no doubt that I'll be reaching out to Everett as my guide again.

Dr. Wayne Pernell
International #1 Bestselling Author, Speaker, and Breakthrough Coach
www.WaynePernell.com

* * *

Everett's kindness, support, and direction make publishing a book a wonderful experience. He helped make There Are No Horseshoes in Heaven an international #1 bestseller. And after it was all said and done, he and his team were right there to help more and more, making the ride even better.

Gratitude all the way!

Carole Herder
International #1 Bestselling Author
Founder & President, Cavallo Inc.

* * *

Let me paint the scene: It's your launch day. The first couple of hours into your book launch are riddled with anxiety. As the day progresses, you get continued updates on the status of your book. Then, the news finally breaks: you have reached #1 in a category. Then another category, and another! Success! All the blood, sweat, and tears that you have put into your book has paid off. As your launch day ends, the process that the team at Ignite Press has so carefully crafted results in your new status as a #1 Bestselling Author.

This story has been my reality on three separate occasions. The entire team at Ignite Press has this down to a science, and I trust them implicitly.

The gift of influence that goes along with being an author is a profit center, privilege, and a responsibility. Use it wisely. Your name and reputation will be written between the pages of your book.

Frank A. Leyes, ChFC
Advisor, Speaker, and #1 International Bestselling Author

* * *

I wrote *Elevate: Self Awareness through Courage, Potential, and Fulfillment* to help bring my message to the world. With the help of Ignite Press, it became a bestseller. Better yet, it became the springboard for our Elevate live events. If you're considering writing a book or launching a product, I would absolutely recommend Ignite Press for at least four reasons: 1) They produce quality work. That was important to me. 2) They are very responsive. You will hear back from them immediately. 3) If you know Everett and his team, they are very authentic and genuine. 4) They get results. It has been a great experience. Thank you Everett and team!

Dr. Keppen Laszlo
Bestselling Author
Director, Discover Health & Wellness Centers

* * *

So you've written a book, or you really want to write a book, and you'd love to be an Amazon #1 bestselling author. And yet, you're afraid you're gonna screw it up. I have you covered. Call Everett O'Keefe at Ignite Press. Everett is the "triple threat" in the life of a book. He's mastered the writing, publishing, and promoting. He launched my book, *Resetology: Calming and Connecting Secrets from the Principal's Office*, and it became a #1 bestseller. He really knows his stuff.

I really wanted to be involved in the launch process. Everett laid out a framework for me, and together, we designed a plan. This allowed me to move forward with peace of mind, knowing the steps ahead of me and that I was working with a proven expert.

During the day of the launch, Everett demonstrated this uncanny knowledge of the inner workings of Amazon. He always knew what was going to happen next. For this reason, I call him "The Book Whisperer"!

I know the phrase is overused, but he really knows his stuff. And we really had an amazingly successful launch day.

I am grateful that Everett took on this project that I care so deeply about, and I knew that I was in the best hands possible. On top of all that, you're just not going to meet a nicer man than Everett O'Keefe. I highly recommend that you work with him and his team.

Jim House
#1 Bestselling Author
Founder of The Book Carver

*   *   *

Everett and his team helped me create and launch *The Happy Mom Mindset* and a workbook to go with it. And I'm so grateful because my book has become one of the very best tools that I have. Working with Everett was so great because I came with the ideas, my energy, and the knowledge of exactly what I wanted. He really helped me to be able to take that and launch it on Facebook and get it out there. I got a ton of traction, became a #1 bestseller, and now I'm able to use it to help people change their lives. And I get emails from people all the time letting me know what a difference the book is making in their lives! I can't thank Everett enough.

Molly Claire
#1 Bestselling Author
Founder, Molly Claire Coaching

*   *   *

When I wrote *The Small Business Owner's Guide to Digital Marketing*, I had a crazy deadline. I wanted the book in my hands in time for a big event at which I was speaking. Frankly, I couldn't have done this without the incredible team at Ignite Press. His team went to work helping fulfill my vision on my timeline, even accommodating my last-minute changes.

I now hand my book out instead of a business card. You should see the looks on people's faces when they ask for a card and get a book instead. It is like magic!

If you are looking to get your book done, get it to market quickly, and work with a fabulous team, you'd be crazy not to work with Everett and the Ignite Press team.

Troy Scott
Speaker and #1 International Bestselling Author
CEO, Complete Online Strategy

* * *

Note: In 2015, Tony Rose unexpectedly lost his 28-year old son. He and his daughter co-wrote a stirring and challenging book called Beautiful Grief, *and it takes a raw, unfiltered look at his and his daughter's journey through mourning. In 2018, Tony and Kate gave us the honor of bringing his book to the world. As we were preparing* the power of the published, *Tony sent us these words:*

My early books really were a calling card. The very fact that you publish a book, I have found, gives you a piece of credibility that others who have not published lack. It does not even matter how good the book is. Saying you have published is a head start. The fact that some might read the book and even endorse the book is terrific but not really that much more powerful. The writing of the book itself is a good way to assess how you process your world. I think that I have always internalized the things I wanted others to understand better by that very process.

The third book that you and I worked on together is a terrific example. I described the concepts of dealing with grief in the way that I was living it but not really conscious of what, exactly, I was doing. Several months after most of the chapters were written, I was confronted, unfortunately, with another situation that was causing me to grieve once again. The organization of my feelings and thinking about grief on paper really helped me understand what I was going through again. I never expected that when I started the writing process.

Finally, I advise that everyone should understand at least one outcome they would anticipate from entering the process of writing a book. My goal was to change just one person's perspective. The byproduct of having an international bestseller was a great accomplishment, but if I helped that one person, that was enough. That happened for me, and one of the several Amazon reviews was from that one person who was moved and helped by the publication of the book. It was worth all the time. It was worth the effort. And it was worth the investment of emotion and intellect. And it really was not that hard when you consider it all.

Tony Rose
#1 International Bestselling Author
Founding Partner, Rose, Snyder & Jacobs

Made in the USA
Monee, IL
06 March 2022